The Log Cabin DESIGN Workbook

Basic Blocks & Beyond

Christal Carter

That Patchwork Place®

Acknowledgments

I am grateful to the students who generously allowed their quilts to be featured here: Vicky Haider, Debbie Myers, and Nancy Ota. Thanks to Kay Lettington for the "bump on a log" name, and special thanks to Barbara Ford for machine quilting several of my quilts and for letting me include her "Galloping Memories" quilt in the book. And, as always, love and thanks to my husband, Bill, for all his assistance.

Dedication

To my children, Carin and Catrina, and to my son-in-law, Brad. This book is a work of love.

Credits

Editor-in-Chief .... Kerry I. Hoffman
Technical Editor .... Janet White
Managing Editor .... Judy Petry
Design Director .... Cheryl Stevenson
Copy Editor .... Liz McGehee
Proofreader .... Melissa Riesland
Illustrator .... Robin Strobel
Illustration Assistant .... Marge Mueller
Photographer .... Brent Kane
Cover Designer .... Kay Green
Text Designer .... Barbara Schmitt
Production Assistant .... Claudia L'Heureux

The Log Cabin Design Workbook: Basic Blocks & Beyond
© 1996 by Christal Carter
That Patchwork Place, Inc., PO Box 118, Bothell, WA 98041-0118 USA

Printed in the United States of America
01 00 99 98 97 96   6 5 4 3 2 1

Library of Congress Cataloging-in-Publication Data
Carter, Christal,
   The log cabin design workbook : basic blocks & beyond / Christal Carter.
     p.   cm.
   ISBN 1-56477-173-3
   1. Patchwork—Patterns. 2. Log cabin quilts. I. Title.
TT835.C3793   1996
746.46'041—dc20
                                   96-31341
                                      CIP

Table of Contents

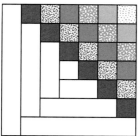

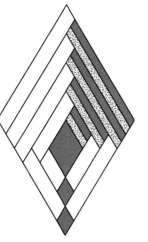

Introduction

For years, I have heard little tidbits of history about the Log Cabin block. Examples of the design date back centuries. One theory suggests the block was derived from land-cultivation methods in Scotland, where the fields were tilled in rows running at right angles to each other to prevent erosion. Another theory says it might have evolved from tile roof patterns on the Isle of Man in the Irish Sea.

I have seen the pattern in tile mosaics and other art forms, but finding an ancient example actually made of fabric was exciting. When I was teaching in Australia, a student showed me a book of pictures from an exhibit of Egyptian antiquities on loan to Canberra from the British Museum. I was astounded! There, in the linen wrappings of a mummified cat, were perfect Log Cabin blocks.

I went on to discover that some of the most interesting historical proof of the Log Cabin design in fabric exists in museums that exhibit Egyptian mummies. Some of these mummified animals with Log Cabin designs as their wrappings date back 2,700 years. While the linen is wrapped rather than sewn, it clearly shows that the Log Cabin design in a fabric format (both Traditional and Courthouse Steps) existed much earlier than I thought.

The fact that the Log Cabin design is a pattern with endless possibilities ensures it will be around for many years to come. I have been designing with it for seventeen years and feel like I am just getting started. I hope this book will open your eyes and imagination to the wondrous things this little block can do.

Since 1979, when I took my first quilting class, I have been making quilts based on the Log Cabin block. At first, I did not particularly like Log Cabin quilts. I was reluctant to make the six required Log Cabin designs, but my teacher was determined that I learn

©British Museum EA6752

"When I was teaching in Australia, a student showed me a book of pictures from an exhibit of Egyptian antiquities on loan to Canberra from the British Museum. I was astounded! There, in the linen wrappings of a mummified cat, were perfect Log Cabin blocks."

the possibilities in this seemingly simple design. Being a rebel at heart, I decided my quilts were going to stand out from the dozens being created in class. I would go farther than the standard Barn Raising or Streak of Lightning settings. My first large Log Cabin quilt was a geometric design I called "Stardance." Next came a series of pictorial quilts with appliquéd details based on the Log Cabin block. Adding appliqué to Log Cabin blocks was considered unusual at that time, so my quilts began to attract some attention. I was off and running.

After authoring three books of Log Cabin pictorial patterns, I decided to do one focusing on the endless variations and fun of designing with the Log Cabin block. In the sections on fabric selection and construction techniques, you will find the basic information you need to select fabric and to speed-piece your Log Cabin blocks. I have not attempted to provide complete instructions on every aspect of quiltmaking. I chose instead to concentrate on the Log Cabin block.

The design section opens the door to the unlimited possibilities of the Log Cabin block, with pages of interesting block variations and setting ideas. And, to start you off on your own Log Cabin design adventures, I have provided design grids that you can copy and use to create your own exciting Log Cabin quilts.

The basic Log Cabin block can be varied in literally thousands of ways: by changing the shape of the center piece, the order of piecing, the color and value combinations, the sizes and types of logs . . . so many variables. My designs have evolved from merely geometric, to complex pictorials, then back to even more elaborate geometric styles. I would like to share some of what I have discovered about that fabulous little block, the Log Cabin.

Designing with the Log Cabin Block

The basic Log Cabin block consists of a center piece surrounded by fabric strips or "logs." It is said that this center piece represents the chimney or hearth of the home. Historically, quilters used red or yellow centers to symbolize the hearth and fire. Tales are told that a Log Cabin quilt with black center squares, hanging on a clothesline or porch during the American Civil War, was a sign of a safe house to runaway slaves. I love that bit of history and plan to make a safe-house quilt for my home soon.

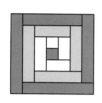

"Tales are told that a Log Cabin quilt with black center squares, hanging on a clothesline or porch during the American Civil War, was a sign of a safe house to runaway slaves."

Block Types and Shapes

The size, shape, and color of the Log Cabin block center piece can vary greatly. Even its position can vary. But as long as logs are added to form the block, it is considered a Log Cabin.

Almost any shape of Log Cabin block can be pieced as either of the two block types: Traditional or Courthouse Steps. The piecing sequence is different for the two types, and the designs formed by each type are different. Traditional blocks are pieced by adding strips in a spiral sequence around the center, proceeding either in a clockwise or counterclockwise direction. Courthouse Steps blocks are pieced by adding successive rounds of strips to opposite sides of the center.

Squares

Squares are the most common and easily recognized Log Cabin blocks. In the following examples, notice that similar fabric values are grouped together in the block, forming triangle-shaped areas of design.

Traditional

Clockwise Piecing

Counterclockwise Piecing

Block appears to be divided into 2 triangles.

Courthouse Steps

Block appears to be divided into 4 triangles.

The size of the center piece can change the design. A center the same size as the logs creates a straight line, while a center that is larger or smaller forms a bump or dip.

Traditional

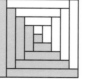

Same-size center   Large center   Small center

Courthouse Steps

Same-size center   Large center   Small center

A center of a different value from either side sets itself apart.

Traditional

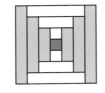
Courthouse Steps

Placing color values in unexpected positions reveals surprising design possibilities.

Traditional

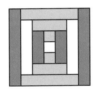

Courthouse Steps

Blocks may have any number of logs, but the most traditional are nine-piece, thirteen-piece, and seventeen-piece blocks.

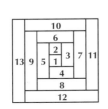

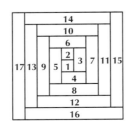

Rectangles

A rectangle is just an elongated square. Both Traditional and Courthouse Steps blocks can be constructed with rectangles. Although they are not as easy to place into settings as squares, rectangles can create interesting designs. If the length of the rectangles is a multiple of the width, you can set alternate rows vertically and horizontally for a woven effect. Use rectangles set side by side or end to end for borders.

Traditional

Courthouse Steps

Rectangles can be set in rows.

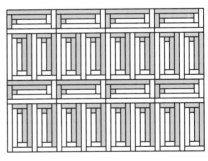

If the block length is a multiple of the block width, you can set them in alternating patterns.

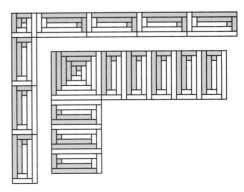

Log Cabin Border Settings

Diamonds

Diamond blocks are similar to squares. Since diamonds also have four sides, they can be made into both block types. But unlike a square, which has four equal angles, a diamond has two *different* angles, which can provide more design possibilities. Notice that the dark- and light-valued areas in traditional Diamond blocks take on different shapes, depending on which way you add the logs.

Diamonds vary in shape, but it's easiest to work with 45° diamonds, which make eight-pointed stars when you sew them together, or 60° diamonds, which make six-pointed stars and hexagonal units.

45° diamond blocks form an eight-pointed star. Fill in with squares and triangles or more diamonds.

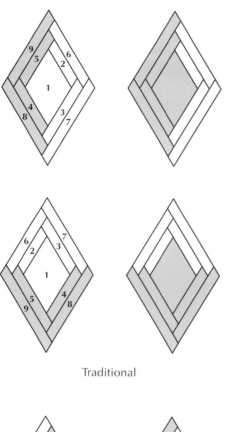

Traditional

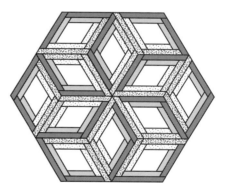

60° diamonds form a six-pointed star. Fill in with more diamonds.

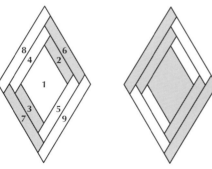

Courthouse Steps

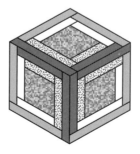

60° diamond blocks make a hexagon or Baby's Block unit.

Other parallelograms (four-sided figures in which the opposite sides are parallel) can be pieced like diamonds, but they don't fit together to form the same larger designs. Diamond blocks have even more design potential than squares.

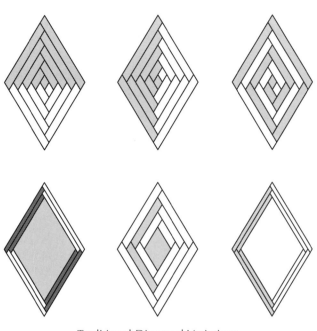

Traditional Diamond Variations

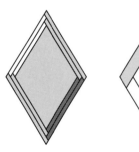

Courthouse Steps Diamond Variations

Triangles

Because triangles have only three sides, you cannot piece them like Courthouse Steps blocks, but you can make many interesting Traditional blocks.

The easiest triangles to set into quilts are half-square triangles, because you can sew them together into squares. I also like equilateral triangles (the length of each side is equal, and each angle is 60°) because they form 60° diamonds, which can be combined to make six-pointed stars, Baby's Block units, or hexagons.

Hexagons

Hexagons, with six sides and 120° angles, give the designer even more possibilities! You can make both Traditional and Courthouse Steps blocks, or you can ignore both of these block types and sew the logs in any order you choose.

45° triangles form squares.

Equilateral triangles form 60° diamonds.

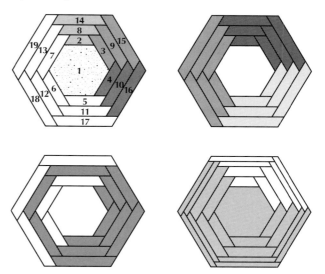

Equilateral Triangle Star

Traditional Hexagon Variations

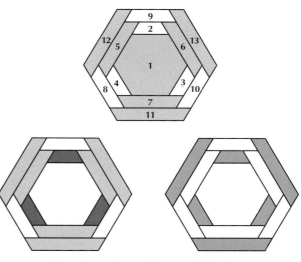

Courthouse Steps Hexagon Variations

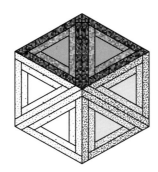

Equilateral Triangle Baby's Block Unit

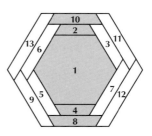

Vary the piecing for different effects.

Pineapple Blocks (Octagons)

The Pineapple block is also considered a type of Log Cabin block. It is really an octagon you can speed-piece like a hexagon.

Pineapple Block

Other Shapes

Almost any angular shape can be used as a center piece for a Log Cabin block, providing it doesn't have an angle greater than 180°. Just remember, odd-shaped blocks are more difficult to sew into settings.

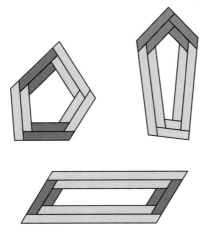

Log Cabin blocks with Odd-Shaped Centers

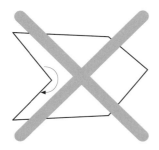

Angle >180°

Designer June Ryker has even devised methods of using bias strips and paper piecing to make curved and elliptical blocks. See "U.F.O." on page 96.

Log Variations

Now that we know what a variety of block shapes can be used, we can explore unusual piecing patterns within the blocks. Many of these variations can be made using either of the Log Cabin piecing methods, so the design possibilities multiply.

Split Log Blocks

By assembling a block the usual way, but using double logs instead of single logs, the logs appear to be split lengthwise. Split Log blocks are easy to make by first strip piecing the double logs, then speed piecing the block. Notice the quilts in the gallery with Split Log blocks: "Woven Hydrangeas"(page 92), "Joy Riding"(page 96), and "Chinese Dragon Dance"(page 89). The widths of the strips making up a log don't need to be the same. You can even try Triple-Split logs.

Split Log Blocks

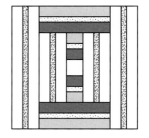

Triple-Split Log Block

Sawed Log Blocks

Make two Log Cabin blocks, cut them in half, and reconnect each half to a different partner for a Sawed Log block. To finish with a square block, you must begin with rectangular blocks to make up for the cut and the seam allowance. Therefore, block centers should be ½" longer than they are wide. This technique works best with square or rectangular blocks.

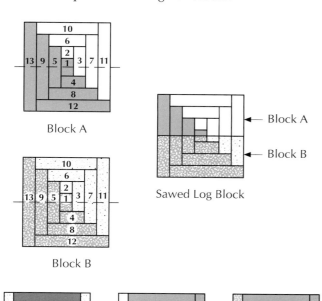

Block A

Block B

Sawed Log Block

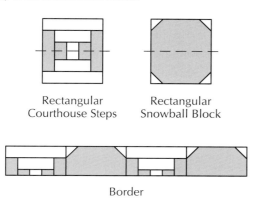

Sawed Log Variations

You can "saw" Log Cabin blocks and use them in other ways too. For example, to make the border of "Holly and the Ivy"(page 91), I halved rectangular Courthouse Steps blocks and rectangular Snowball blocks, then alternated them.

Rectangular Courthouse Steps

Rectangular Snowball Block

Border

Rounded Blocks

Rounded blocks are Traditional blocks, usually squares or rectangles, with corners replaced by triangles, producing the illusion of a curved shape.

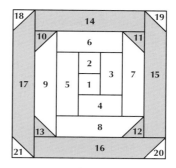

Rounded Block

Off-Center Blocks

In an Off-Center block, the center piece is not in the true center of the block because the number of logs on each side is not equal. Sometimes, one or more sides of the block has no logs at all!

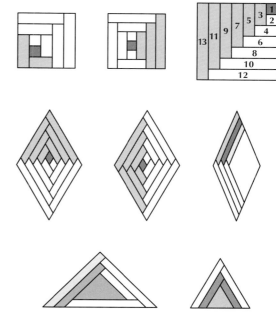

Off-Center Blocks

Off-Center blocks can help you place a design element where you need it. For example, I made Off-Center blocks for the eyes of the bear in "Toytime Teddy" (page 93) so they would appear in the correct positions on the face.

Lopsided Blocks

Lopsided blocks are sometimes called Off-Center blocks. They are blocks with an equal number of logs on each side of the center, but because the logs of two adjacent sides are of different widths than the logs on the other two sides, the blocks appear lopsided, resulting in a curved effect. See "Woven Hydrangeas" on page 92 and "Cat Food" on page 93.

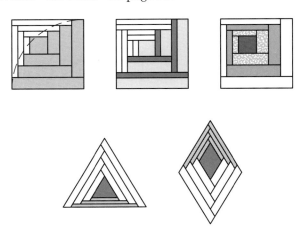

Lopsided Blocks

Chimneys and Cornerstones Blocks

Chimneys and Cornerstones is an old block pattern. Logs contain an extra square piece—a chimney or cornerstone—that adds an interesting geometric component. Chimneys can cross the block in one or two directions. See "Chimneys and Cornerstones II" on page 89.

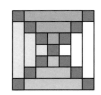

Chimneys and Cornerstones Variations

See "Elephant Walk" on page 89 and "Maple Leaf" on page 95 for examples of diamond chimneys and cornerstones. The Colorado Star Log Cabin setting on page 29 is a square Chimneys and Cornerstones block with diamond-shaped cornerstones attached to the last round of logs only. When blocks are sewn together, the diamonds form an eight-pointed star. There are other variations of this block type with names like "Corners in the Cabin" and "Goose in the Cabin."

Note that on a 90° triangle block, chimneys can be squares, triangles, or diamonds.

There is another type of Cornerstone block I call "knots in the logs." These blocks contain some normal logs and some full of knots or small squares. Both Traditional and Courthouse Steps blocks can have knots. I devised this block to make more realistic ears of corn for my "Pumpkin Frost" quilt in *Quilts for All Seasons*.

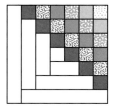

Knots in the Logs

Crazy Log Blocks

Strips that vary in width make fun and easy blocks. Making these Crazy Log blocks is a good way to use up irregular scraps. Add strips to the center until the block is slightly larger than the required size, then trim to the desired dimensions. The center can be any shape.

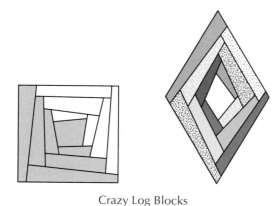

Crazy Log Blocks

Pleated Log Blocks

Pleated Log Cabin quilts were plentiful around the turn of the century. They are visually appealing because of their textured look. Originally, Pleated Log blocks were made by sewing each log directly to the batting and backing, then tediously assembling them. I devised a Semi-Pleated block that looks like the antique one but requires less work. You can speed-piece these blocks just like any other Log Cabin block; only the pressing is different. See the directions for Semi-Pleated blocks on page 72.

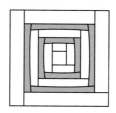

Semi-Pleated Block

Chopped Log Blocks

Chopped Log blocks have many pieces. Cut a strip-pieced unit into logs to create a chopped appearance. See "Tribute to the Arts" on page 95. The dark pinwheel in the center of the quilt is composed of Chopped Log blocks with pleats.

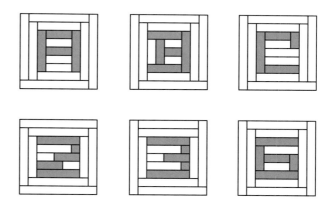

A strip-pieced unit is sliced into logs.

Alphabet and Number Blocks

The Log Cabin block can be adapted to make alphabet and number blocks so you can personalize your quilt with text. See "Toytime Teddy" on page 93 and piecing instructions for alphabet and number blocks on pages 73–75.

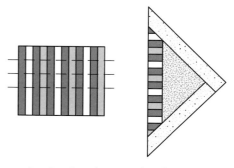

Combination Blocks

There are countless ways to combine the block types and their variations, and different blocks can often be combined to create unusual quilt designs.

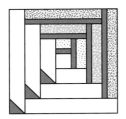

Traditional Split Log (2 sides only) with triangular chimneys

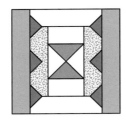

Courthouse Steps with pieced center and thorns

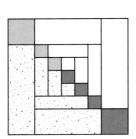

Traditonal with varied-size logs and chimneys

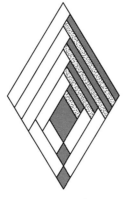

Off-Center Split Log (1 side only) Courthouse Steps block with chimneys

Block Embellishments

Beading, embroidery, ribbons, Prairie Points, and more add to the fun and interest of a quilt. While most beading and embroidery is done when the quilt top is complete, I enjoy machine embroidering decorative stitches along a fabric strip even before piecing it into the block.

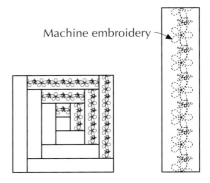

Machine embroidery

Prairie Points add a distinctive design element. Insert them as you add strips to a block to make "thorny" logs.

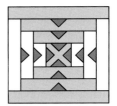

Thorny Logs

Other insertions with more rounded shapes I call "bumps on a log." They can be lace or scallops of fabric. Self-faced scallops could become ears, petals, or leaves. Just pin in place before adding the next log. Press the seam toward the outside to make the "bumps" face in; press the seam toward the center to make the "bumps" face out.

Scallop   Leaf

Insert as you add the top log.

Center pieces for any block can be made of two or more pieces. See "Elephant Walk" on page 89 and "Spool Box" on page 91.

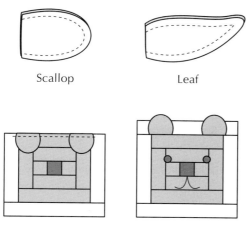

Pictorial Designs

If you are familiar with my work, you know that pictorial quilts are my favorite types of Log Cabin designs. I find it challenging to create a good pictorial design within the confines of the Log Cabin block. By adding appliqué and embroidery, I can achieve more detail than the Log Cabin format allows. Appliqué also softens the geometric lines of the logs.

The pictorial patterns included in this book are based on square and diamond blocks, but all block shapes can be used pictorially. To create large pictorial designs like "Toytime Teddy" (page 93), use square blocks. Begin with ordinary graph paper (the kind with a plain grid—not the kind with two colors of ink or two sizes of lines).

Because square Traditional blocks and Courthouse Steps blocks are pieced so they appear to make triangle shapes, use them in your design as if they *are* triangles.

The blocks actually look like this:

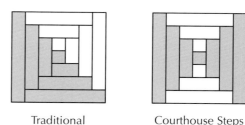

Traditional   Courthouse Steps

But pretend they look like this:

Traditional   Courthouse Steps

Create a design on graph paper, working as if each square is a block that can be divided into triangles or left whole. Just remember, when designing Log Cabin quilts, *each tiny square on the graph paper will become a block,* so don't use too many squares! Check the chart at right to decide how many squares to work with.

Follow any line on the graph paper, or divide any square using the triangular shapes of the Log Cabin blocks. Divide squares from corner to corner at a 45° angle. Do not divide squares horizontally or vertically. When you make these little squares into Log Cabin blocks, the diagonal lines will actually be "stairsteps" composed of individual logs. For now, ignore that.

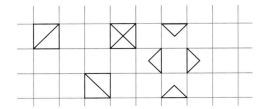

Graph squares can be divided like any of these.

Begin to draw on the graph paper. Below is a simple house and pine tree design. Once you learn some Log Cabin variations, you can add details to the design. That is where special Log Cabin "graph paper" or design grids can be of help. See pages 77–88.

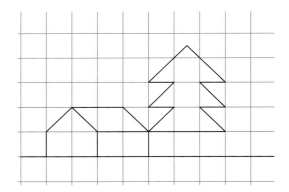

Draw simple lines on graph paper to begin the design.

To determine the quilt size and which size blocks you will use (nine-, thirteen- or seventeen-piece blocks), see the chart below. Notice that a small increase in the width of the strips can make a big difference in the finished size of the block. Wide strips reduce the intricacy of the design, so for most pictorials, use 1"- or 1¼"-wide strips.

Finished Size for Square Log Cabin Blocks

	NUMBER OF PIECES PER BLOCK		
	9	13	17
UNFINISHED STRIP WIDTH	FINISHED BLOCK SIZE		
1"	2½"	3½"	4½"
1¼"	3¾"	5¼"	6¾"
1½"	5"	7"	9"
1¾"	6¼"	8¾"	11¼"

To calculate the finished quilt size, use these formulas:
width = number of blocks across x finished block size
length = number of blocks down x finished block size

Use Log Cabin design grids (pages 77–88) to design unusual pieced blocks. Decide which block type (Traditional or Courthouse Steps) will work best for each unusual block. For the little house design, you might want to make a detailed graph of the window block. I think a Courthouse Steps block works best for a window, so I use a thirteen-piece Courthouse Steps graph-paper block to draw it in detail. Would you like to add a chimney or a curlicue of smoke? Make a spiral block. Work on these variations once the basic design is conceived. You may even want to draw your own block from scratch and change the piecing order entirely to get the design you need.

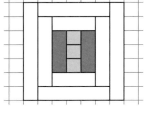

Window with shutters

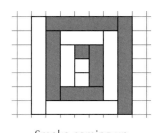

Smoke coming up from a chimney

The next step is to create a work sheet. Color the graph-paper design with colored pencils, then count and categorize the blocks for ease of speed piecing. Color special blocks on Log Cabin graph paper, cut them out, and tape them along the edge of your work sheet.

Before piecing the blocks, you need to make a few more design decisions. A Traditional block can be divided into two triangles, but if you look closely, you will notice the triangles are slightly different in size. One half of the block is always larger, the half that contains the center and has the last logs pieced. Use the larger half of the block for the more important part of the picture. On this design, the roof is more important than the sky, so the roof should use the larger half of the block. Notice that in pictorials, the block center is kept the same size as the logs so the diagonal line across the block is straight. See page 5.

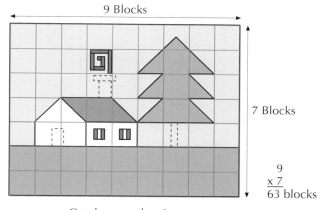

9 Blocks

7 Blocks

9
x 7
63 blocks

Graph paper drawing
(Dotted lines indicate appliqué.)

Detail Blocks

Make 1 smoke.   Make 2 windows.

1	■	Brown (roof)
2	□	White (house)
26	□	Blue (sky)
21	▨	Green (grass and tree)
6	◩	Green/blue (tree and sky)
1	◩	Brown/blue (roof and sky)
1	◢	Brown/white (roof and house)
1	◩	White/blue (roof and sky)
1	▷	Green/blue (tree top)

60 standard blocks + 3 detail blocks = 63
(number of blocks above should equal this number)

When you set up your work sheet, draw the Traditional blocks so the bigger half sits as if it were a capital L. The smaller half is in the 7 position on the upper right of each square. This way, you know by looking at the work sheet that the brown is the bigger half, and you must begin these blocks with a brown center.

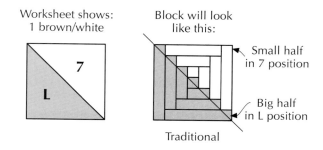

Worksheet shows:
1 brown/white

7

L

Block will look
like this:

Small half
in 7 position

Big half
in L position

Traditional

The same unequal division occurs with the Courthouse Steps block. Notice that two of the triangles are larger than the other two. You must decide which part of the block to use in the design. Draw the Courthouse Steps blocks on the work sheet, placing the larger triangles on the sides and the smaller triangles at the top and bottom. Write the color of the larger triangles first.

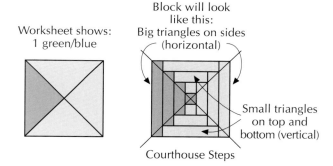

Worksheet shows:
1 green/blue

Block will look
like this:
Big triangles on sides
(horizontal)

Small triangles
on top and
bottom (vertical)

Courthouse Steps

If the whole square is one color, you can make either block type. When all the logs in a block are the same color and value, the piecing sequence doesn't matter. When the piecing sequence is unimportant, make Courthouse Steps blocks since they are faster to construct. See speed piecing of Courthouse Steps blocks on pages 68–69.

One of the wonderful things about Log Cabin blocks in a pictorial format is how easily you can change the size of the quilt without changing the design. For a small version of the design, use nine-piece blocks with 1"-wide strips. To enlarge, make thirteen-piece blocks or use wider strips; the overall design remains the same. However, you can get more detail with a seventeen-piece block than with a nine-piece block.

Use appliqué when you need unusual shapes in the design or when a bit of softening is called for. Here are some examples of pictures you can make with only a few blocks and a minimal amount of appliqué.

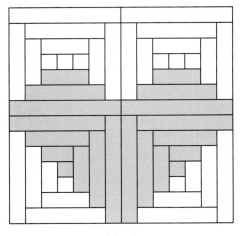

Heart

Rose

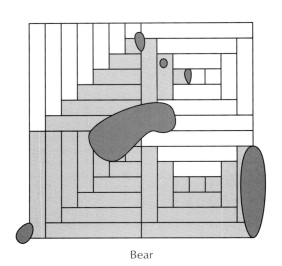

Bear

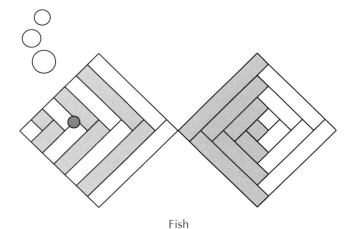

Fish

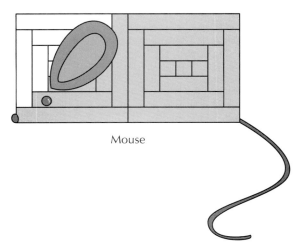

Mouse

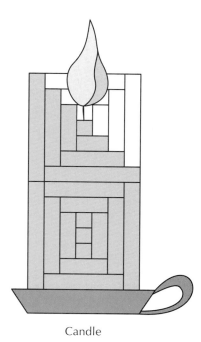

Candle

You can create pictorial designs from other shapes besides squares. See "Cat Dance in the Haystacks" on page 95. Instead of graph paper with a square grid, use graph paper with equilateral triangles to design with triangles, diamonds, or hexagons in the same manner as for squares, but with even more possibilities.

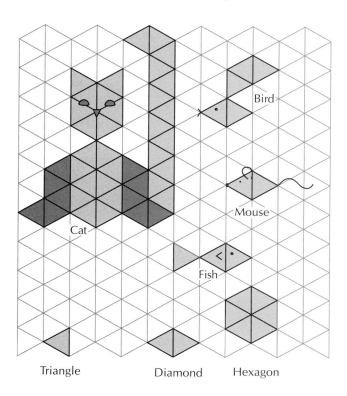

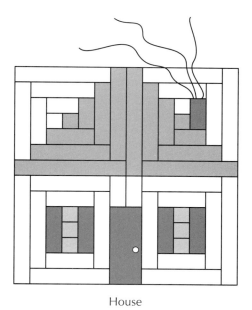

House

Blocks and Settings

The following pages contain examples of Log Cabin block settings and borders. Copy and color them to create personalized quilt plans. Design your own Log Cabin blocks and quilts using the block grids on pages 77–88. I copy and cut them apart to try putting blocks together in new and interesting ways.

Traditional blocks are arranged in a Barn Raising setting.

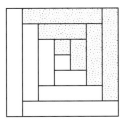

*Courthouse Steps blocks are combined
in this Sunshine and Shadows setting.*

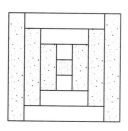

Traditional blocks with a small center are arranged in a Barn Raising setting.

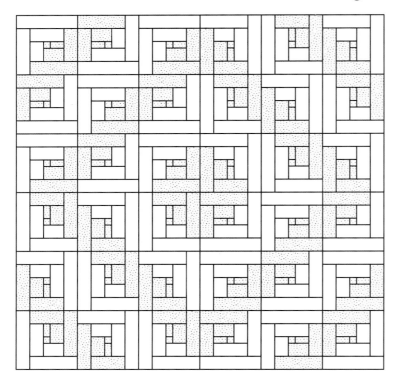

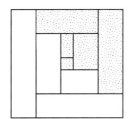

Courthouse Steps blocks combine to form elongated spiral pinwheels.

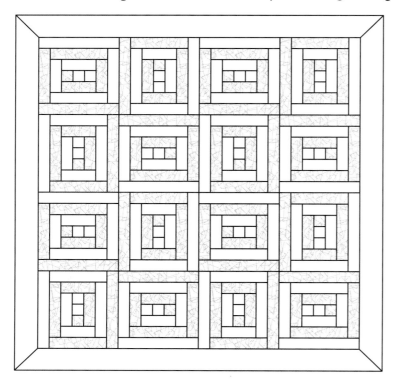

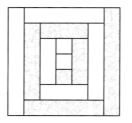

Traditional blocks with a large center are combined in a Straight Furrows setting. In this time-honored setting, notice how the large center creates a "bump" along the diagonal.

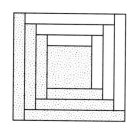

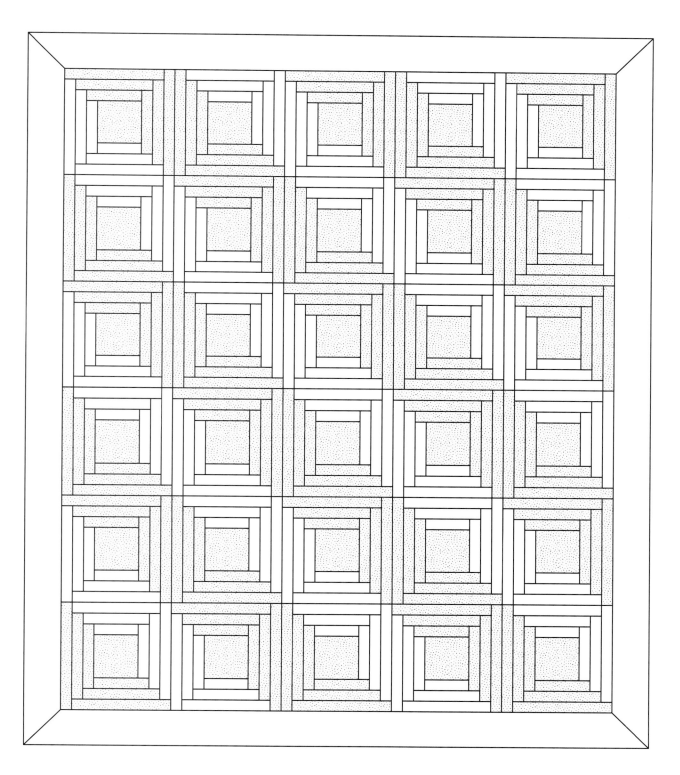

Offset Courthouse Steps blocks create a horizontal Streak of Lightning setting. Large centers are strip-pieced.

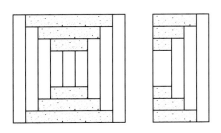

Lopsided Traditional blocks are arranged in a
Sunshine and Shadows setting with sashing.

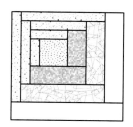

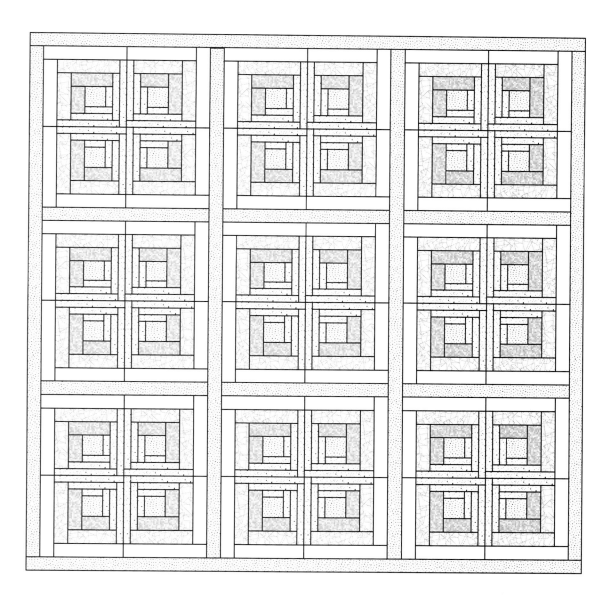

Lopsided Traditional blocks add a twist to this Barn Raising setting.

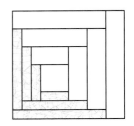

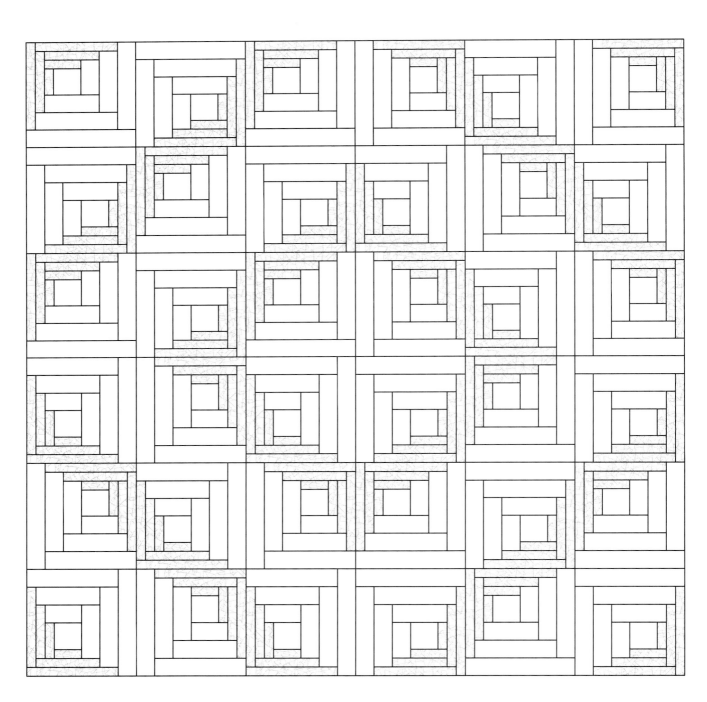

Lopsided blocks and "knots in the log" blocks in a Barn Raising setting resemble the Trip Around the World pattern.

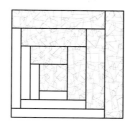
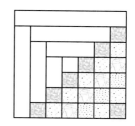

One- and two-directional Chimneys and Cornerstones blocks create an unusual Barn Raising variation.

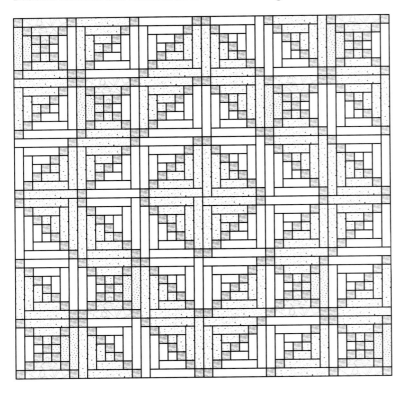
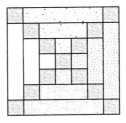
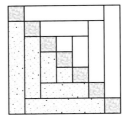

Courthouse Steps blocks are combined with Chimneys and Cornerstones.

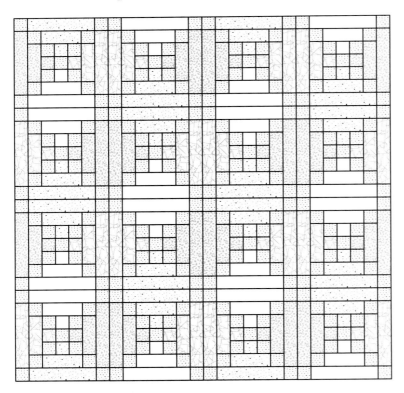
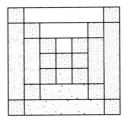

Diamonds at outer block corners form stars in the Barn Raising setting of this Colorado Star Log Cabin design.

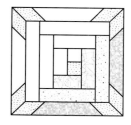

Crazy Log blocks create a
contemporary Barn Raising.

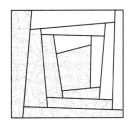

Crazy Logs appear to form a lattice.

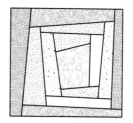

*Split Log Courthouse Steps blocks alternate
directions in a side-by-side setting.*

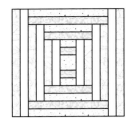

Split Log blocks are arranged in a
Straight Furrows setting.

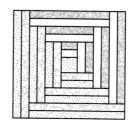

Split Log blocks combine to form this striking grid.

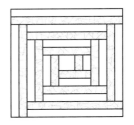

Sawed Log Traditional blocks are set with sashing.

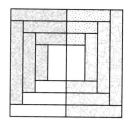

Sawed Log Traditional blocks make a Sunshine and Shadows variation.

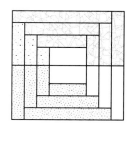

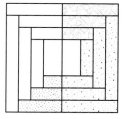

Sawed Log Courthouse Steps blocks combine to form pinwheels. Circles are appliquéd.

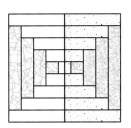

Two types of Off-Center blocks combine

in this easy geometric design.

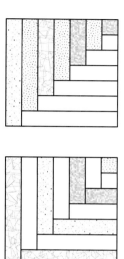

Easy Off-Center Split Log blocks make a striking geometric grid.

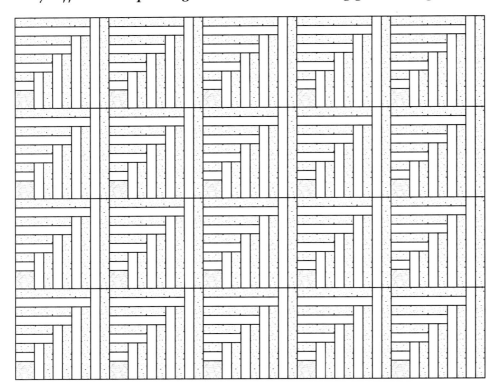
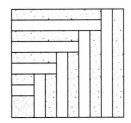

Unusual Off-Center blocks create a woven look.

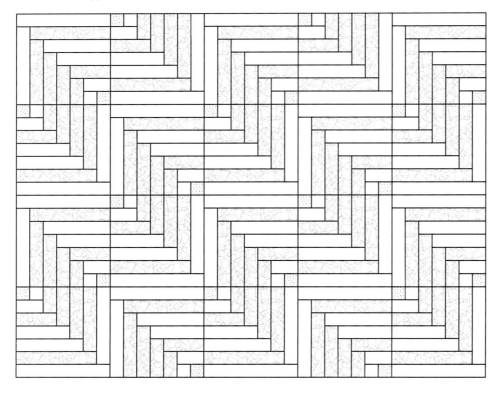
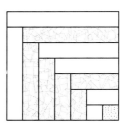

Two types of Pineapple blocks create this unusual setting.

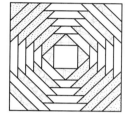

Courthouse Steps blocks are combined with Prairie Points—a "thorny logs" design.

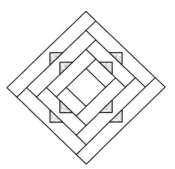

Traditional Diamond blocks create a three-dimensional design.

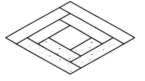

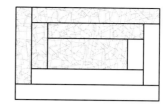

Rectangular Traditional blocks are combined in this Streak of Lightning setting.

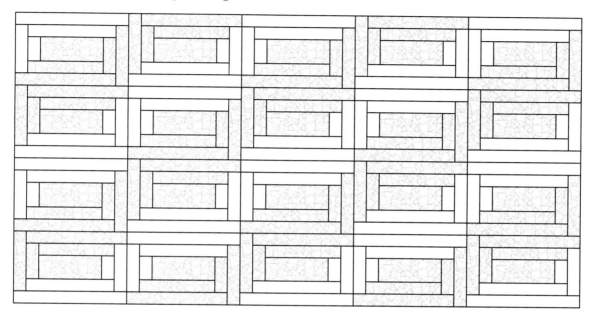

Rectangular Traditional and Courthouse Steps blocks create an unusual design.

Rectangular Courthouse Steps blocks create this woven design.

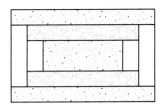

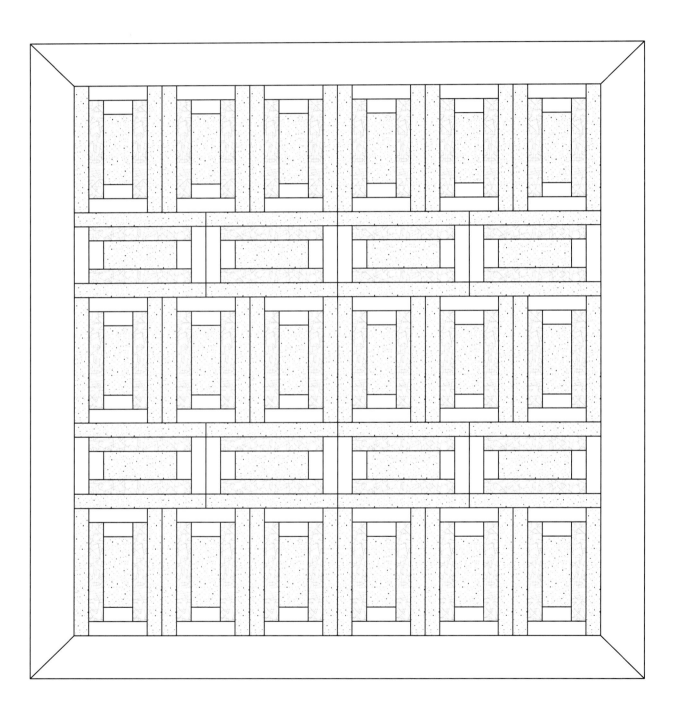

*Blocks start as rectangles; square them up
with an extra piece to form a pinwheel.*

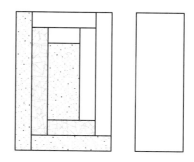

Off-Center Diamond blocks, Traditional Triangle blocks, and Half-Square Triangle blocks create a medallion design.

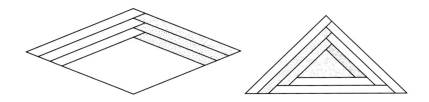

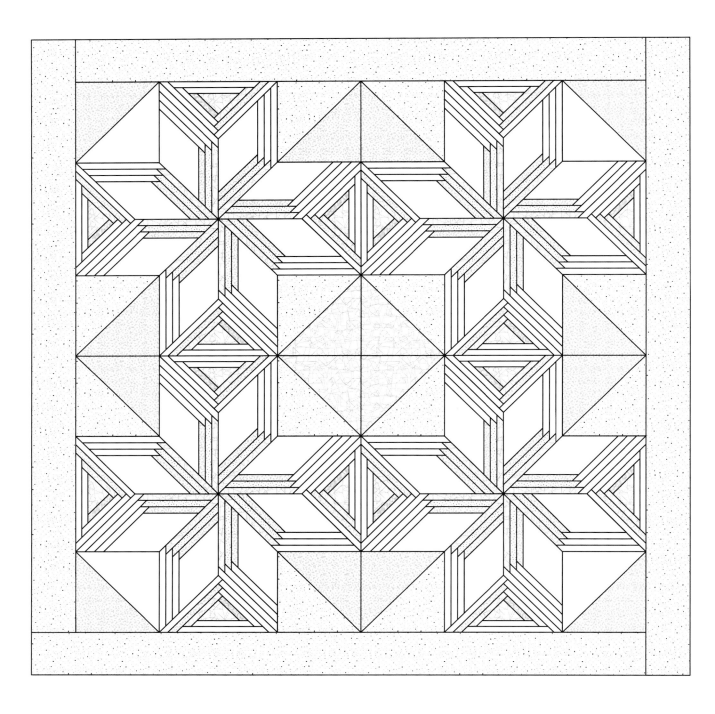

Off-Center Diamond blocks form eight-pointed stars. Half-Square Triangle blocks fill in.

*Split Log Off-Center Diamond blocks create
a three-dimensional lattice design.*

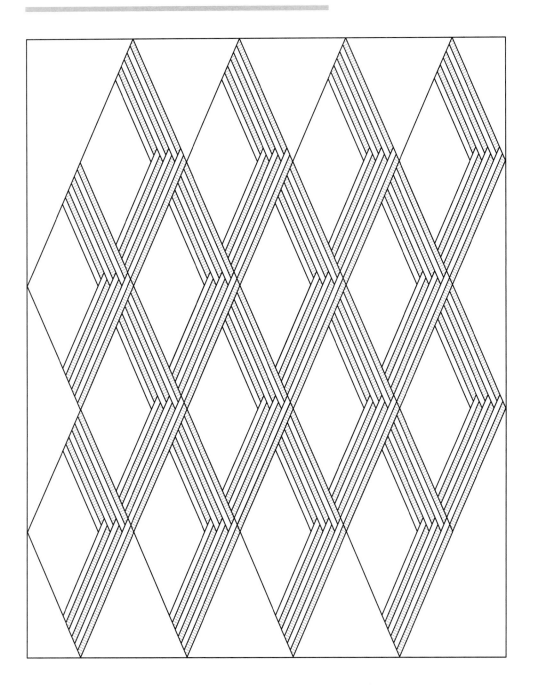

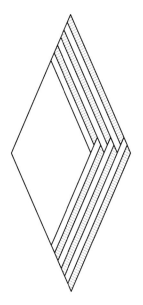

60° Split Log Diamond blocks form a star. More diamonds fill in to form a hexagon.

Diamond blocks with Chimneys and Cornerstones form a six-pointed star. Split Log Diamond blocks fill in.

Split Log Diamond blocks and Off-Center Triangle blocks make a star. Diamond-shaped Chimneys and Cornerstones blocks form a hexagonal frame.

Three 60° diamonds combine to form the centers of these hexagonal Log Cabin blocks. Using different fabric values creates three-dimensional Baby's Blocks.

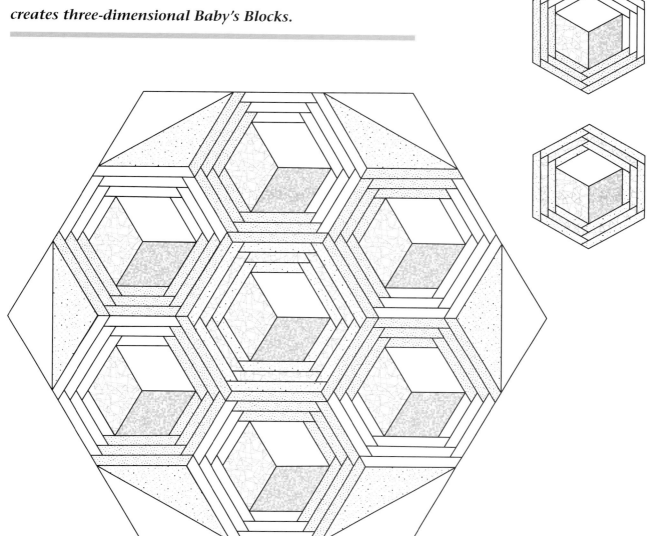

Triangle blocks form hexagonal pinwheels inside a larger hexagon.

Equilateral Triangle blocks are arranged in a zigzag diamond setting.

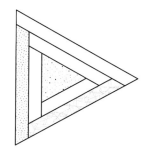

Equilateral Triangle blocks make three large diamonds.

Fill in with large equilateral triangles.

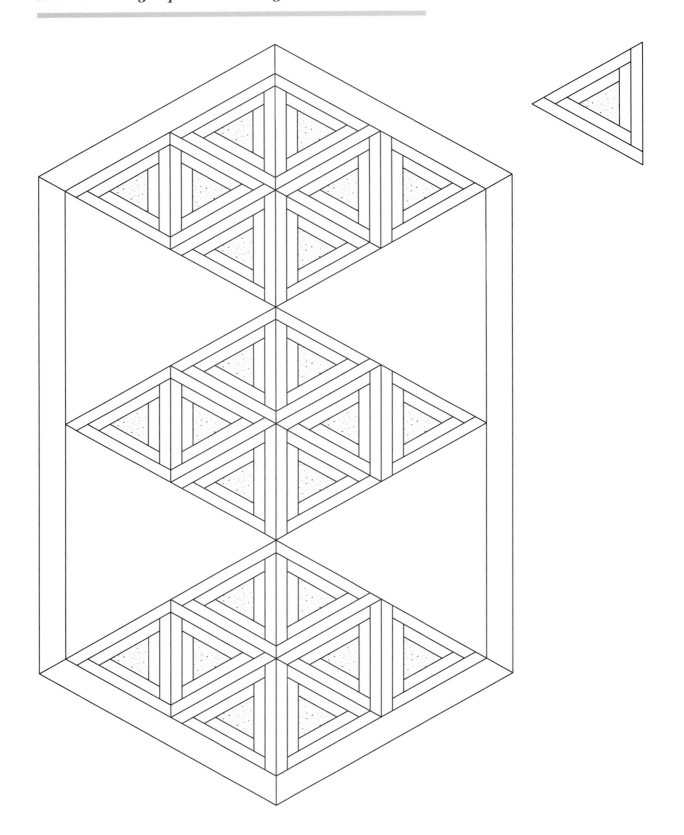

An eight-pointed star is formed using 45° Triangle blocks. Half-Square Triangle blocks fill in.

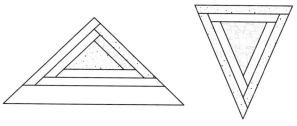

Triangle block stars are repeated in this design.

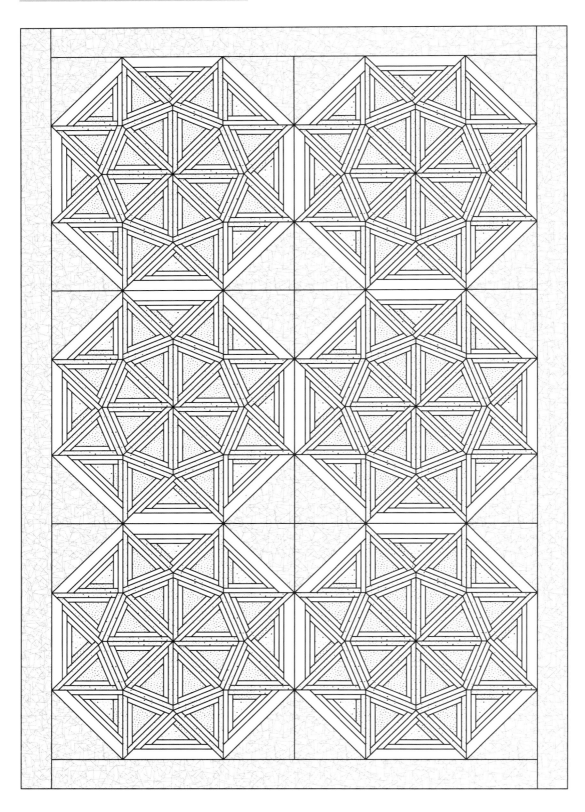

***Split Log Half-Square Triangle blocks
create a floating lattice.***

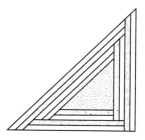

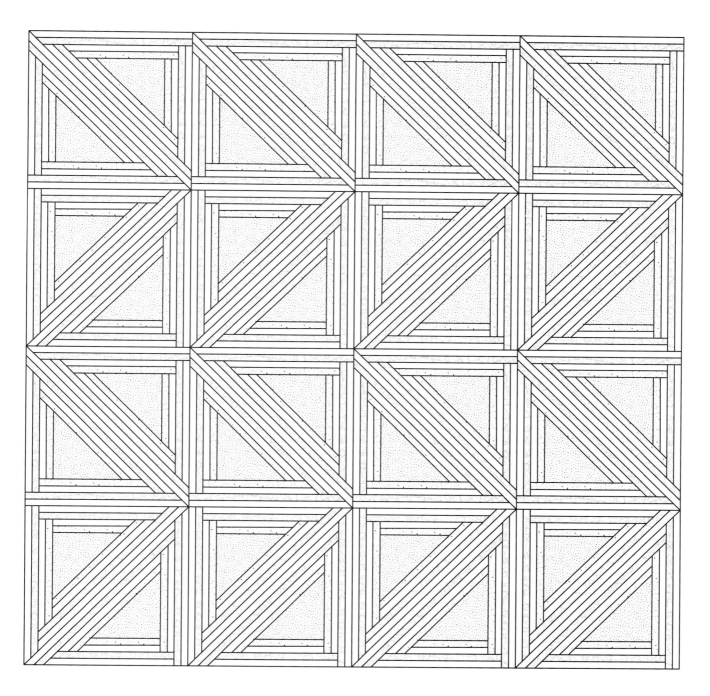

Traditional Hexagon blocks with strip-pieced diamonds and triangles make a dramatic design.

Hexagonal Log Cabin blocks create a wonderful medallion.

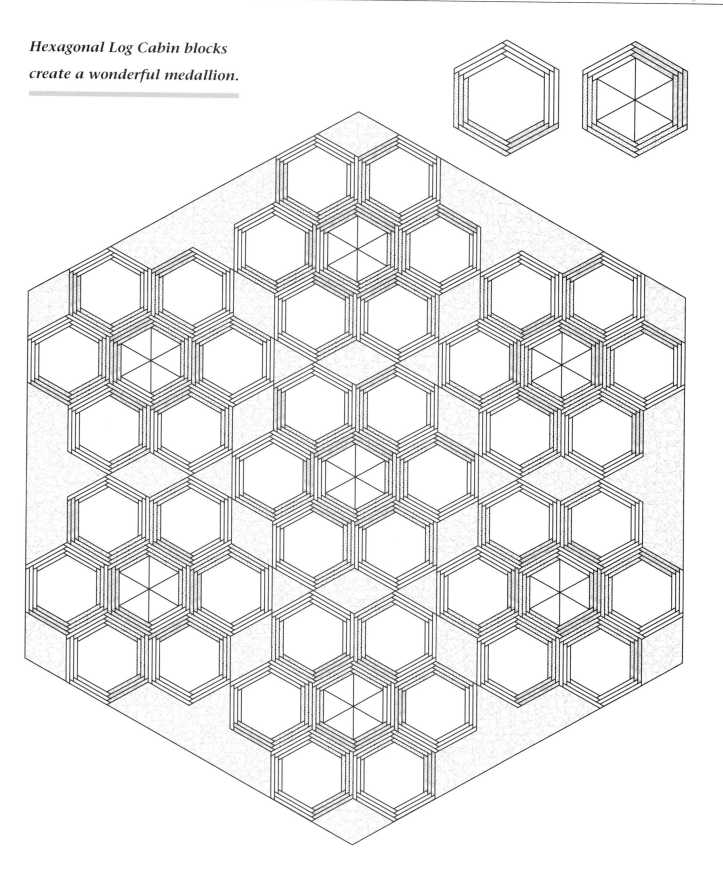

Log Cabin Borders

Traditional blocks

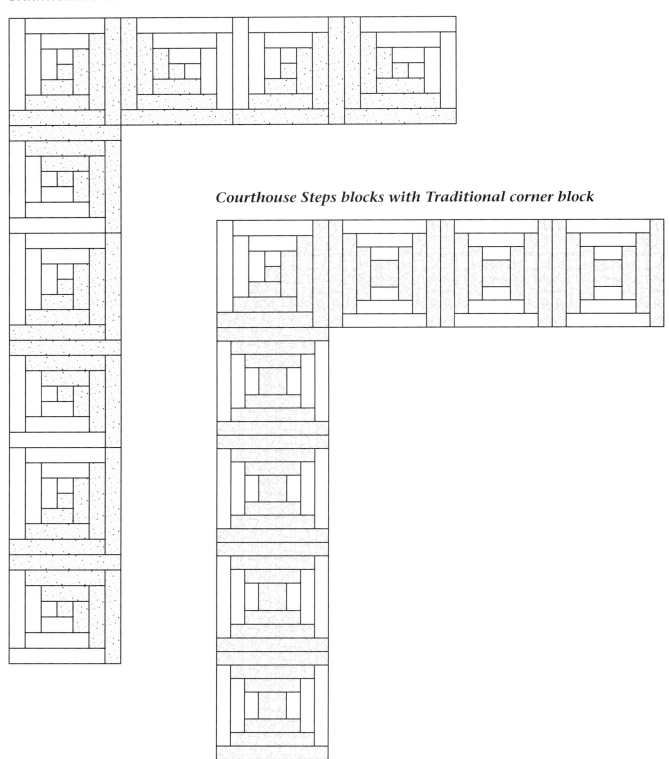

Courthouse Steps blocks with Traditional corner block

Courthouse Steps elongated spiral blocks

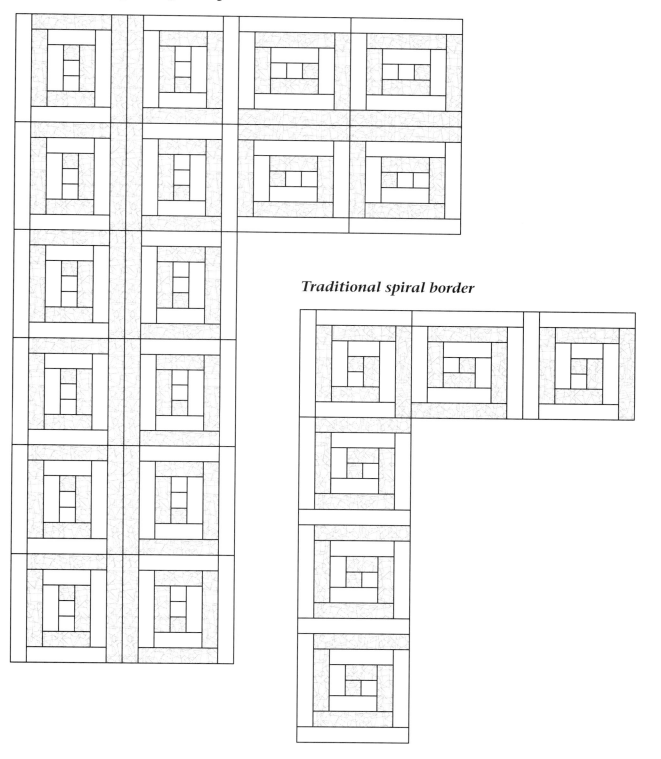

Traditional spiral border

One- and two-directional Chimneys and Cornerstones blocks

Split Log Traditional and Courthouse Steps blocks

Courthouse Steps with "thorny logs"

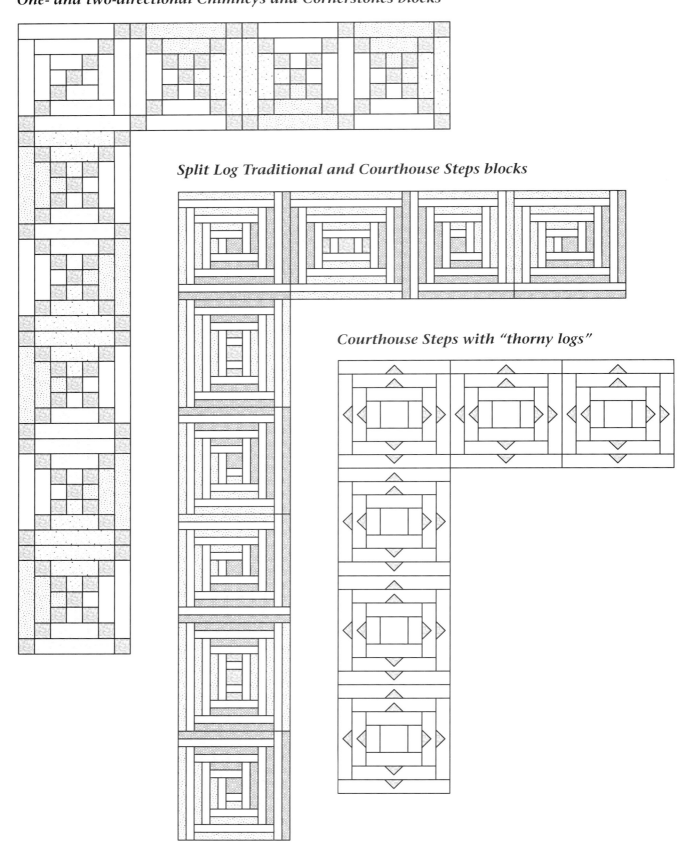

Sawed Log Courthouse Steps blocks with an Off-Center corner block

Traditional blocks with Attic Window centers and two rounded corners

Sawed Log Courthouse Steps blocks with a strip-pieced corner square

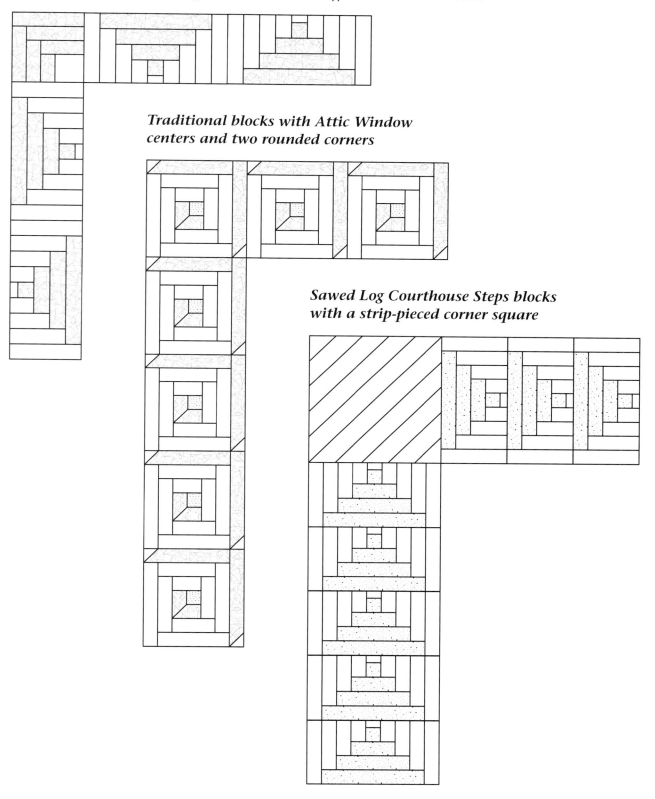

Off-Center Diamond blocks

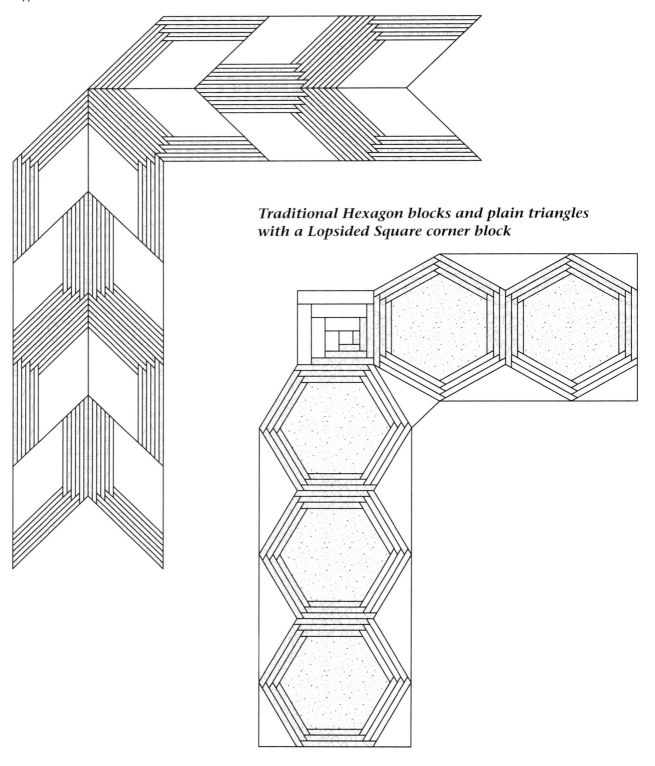

Traditional Hexagon blocks and plain triangles with a Lopsided Square corner block

Templates
Use any size of these shapes as centers for blocks.

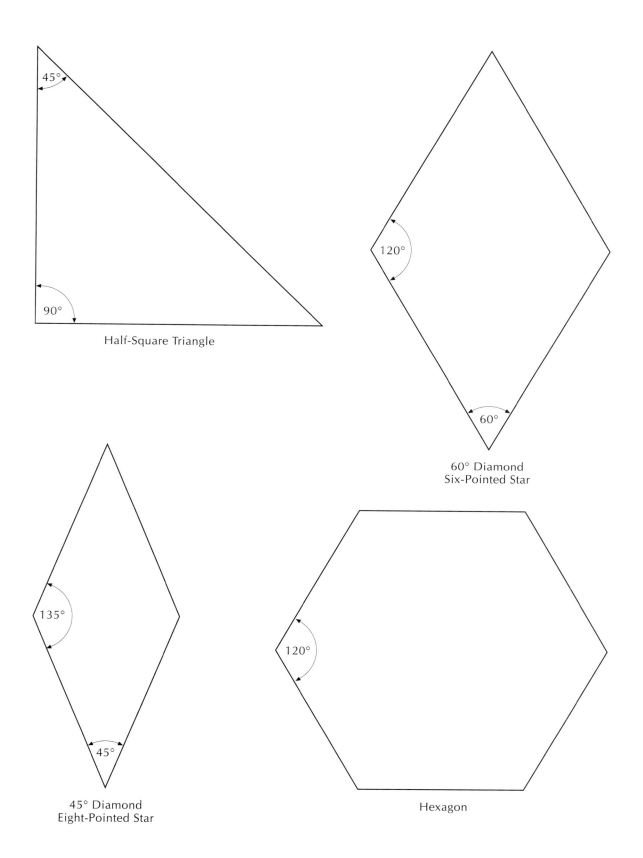

Half-Square Triangle

60° Diamond
Six-Pointed Star

45° Diamond
Eight-Pointed Star

Hexagon

Fabric Selection

In general, I recommend using 100% cotton fabrics for your quilts. All the fabrics for a quilt should be similar in weight and texture and also colorfast.

For hand appliqué and blind-stitch machine appliqué, I also prefer 100% cotton because it is easy to fold the raw edges under. Cotton blends work well for machine appliqué with a satin-stitched edge, because the edges do not need to be turned under. In fact, a permanent-press blend may be preferable if the finished item will be washed frequently.

Sometimes I break the rules by using a more exotic fabric, such as lamé in "On Stage" (page 92), felt in "Log Cabin in the Woods" (page 90), or silk and satin in "Resurrection" (page 94). Take precautions with these unusual fabrics, especially if you are a novice quiltmaker. Velvet, for example, is really too heavy to combine with cotton in tiny Log Cabin blocks, yet on occasion, I have done just that. Felt is too thick to be traditionally pieced, but is wonderful for appliqué or special piecing techniques. Go ahead and be creative; just use a bit of caution.

There are so many wonderful fabrics available at relatively reasonable prices. You can make geometric Log Cabin blocks using any of the various fabric designs available, from large-scale to tiny prints. "Elephant Walk" (page 89) features a wonderful large-scale print, while "Strawberries and Tea"(page 90) is composed of tiny-scale florals.

For Log Cabin picture designs, I use solids and small- to medium-size prints that contain few colors. Very busy or large-scale prints complicate the design and draw attention to themselves. It is best if the eye is drawn to the overall picture rather than to an individual fabric within the picture. The strips used in pictorial designs are very narrow and often, with a large multicolor print, the color you wished to emphasize is not even contained in the strip. When this happens, the block will not read as a homogenous color and will mar the picture you are trying to create.

When you are making a pictorial Log Cabin quilt, deciding what fabrics to include in each color group is very important. You want the groups to read as if they are a solid unit. For example, each object (bear, balloons, block, and car) in "Toytime Teddy" (page 93) consists of a group of fabrics in different values of the same color. The variety of fabrics is different enough to

show off the piecing, yet not so different that the bear or the balloon looks choppy. The key is to achieve unity in value (darkness or lightness of a color) as you combine fabrics that are just different enough so all the little pieces show.

To group fabrics by value, stack fabrics of each color group together, overlapping the folded edges by ½" (the width of the finished strips in most pictorial Log Cabin quilts), then look at the group from a distance. If one of the fabrics sticks out, discard it or move it to another value group.

For a geometric (nonpictorial) design, you can choose from a much wider variety of fabrics. Feel free to experiment with a wide range of colors, prints, values, and scales.

Stripes, for example, are especially interesting in Log Cabin piecing. I usually cut across the stripe to avoid the appearance of crooked logs. Sometimes, however, I cut along the stripe to make the logs appear strip pieced without extra sewing.

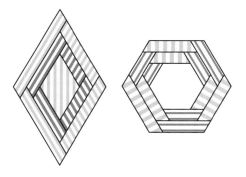

Large-scale prints can be used for fussy-cut block centers. These prints also bring movement and interest to simple, straight logs. Different prints of the same colors and values will blur the divisions between the logs and result in a softer look.

Construction Techniques

Cutting

The rotary cutter will easily cut through four to six layers of fabric. Clean and oil your cutter before you begin a new project. (Be sure to wipe off any excess oil before cutting your fabric.)

Use your rotary ruler to measure and cut strips. For consistent blocks, use the same ruler throughout a project. Do not use the grid lines on the mat to measure strip widths, since they are not as accurate as a ruler. Instead, use them to square up the fabric. Lay the fold of the fabric along a horizontal line on the cutting mat and place the rotary ruler along a vertical line, keeping the ruler perpendicular to the fold.

I fold my fabric only once (as it comes on the bolt) and cut strips on the crosswise grain. You can stack and cut two or three fabrics at the same time. Avoid folding fabric more than once or twice; too many folds can result in crooked strips.

Folding like this:

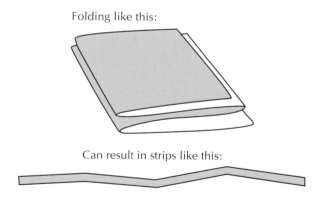

Can result in strips like this:

There is no need to mark fabrics; simply run the rotary cutter along the ruler edge. (If the strip is still attached here and there, the blade may be nicked; replace it with a new one.)

As you sew strips together, look for any that seem to be wider or narrower than the rest. Discard these strips, since they will result in blocks that are too small or too large.

In general, it takes one strip of fabric (1" x 44") to make one thirteen-piece block or two nine-piece blocks. This guideline may help you calculate the yardage for a Log Cabin project. If a pattern calls for twelve thirteen-piece blocks, you will need 12" of fabric. If the blocks are made of two different fabrics, you will need 6" of each and so on.

Using Templates

For square blocks, make plastic templates for squaring and sizing. Compare the template with your finished blocks to make sure they are of uniform size.

To make diamond, triangle, or hexagon Log Cabin blocks, you will need accurate center templates for those shapes. Some center templates are included on page 63. Trace them onto template plastic to experiment with the different shapes. But to make an entire project, buy thick acrylic templates, like the rotary rulers, because you will use them with a rotary cutter.

Pressing

I recommend that you press as you sew. This is especially important with tiny blocks, such as those in pictorials, and imperative when using irregular shapes, such as diamonds and hexagons. I always use a dry iron because my fingers are so close to the pressing—steamed fingers are painful. Since you need to press often during the piecing process, keep your ironing board close.

Press seam allowances toward the outside of the block. This rule applies to all Traditional or Courthouse Steps blocks of any shape. Press after adding each strip, pressing toward the uncut strip just added.

Blocks should not be stretched while pressing, but they must be pressed all the way out to prevent pleats or tucks in the logs. Otherwise, the blocks will be too small. To ensure proper pressing with no pleats, always press on the right side (or top) of the blocks before trimming the most recently added strip.

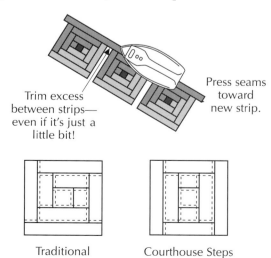

Trim excess between strips—even if it's just a little bit!

Press seams toward new strip.

Traditional   Courthouse Steps

For unusual blocks, you may break the pressing rules. For Sawed Log blocks, press the seam allowances of half the rectangle blocks toward the outside in the normal manner. Press the seam allowances of the other half of the blocks toward the centers. When you "saw" the blocks in half and sew each half together with a new partner, the seam allowances of each half will go in opposite directions, and the block will be flatter.

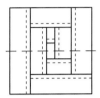 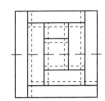

Pressing a block with "thorns" or bumps can vary, depending on which way you want the thorn to face. For thorns facing the center of the block, press seams *away from* the center. If you want the thorns facing toward the outside of the block, press the seams *toward* the center.

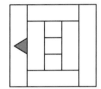 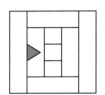

Press seam toward center for "thorn" to point out.

Press seam toward outside for "thorn" to point in.

Speed Piecing

I always use speed-piecing techniques to make my Log Cabin quilts because it saves time. Use speed piecing whenever there are several of each block type and color combination required.

Before beginning to speed-piece the blocks, it is a good idea to make a sample block. A sample enables you to check strip width, seam allowances, and finished block size. Make sure all seam allowances are exactly ¼" wide. If you have a special ¼" foot for your machine, use it.

The two basic types of Log Cabin blocks are Traditional and Courthouse Steps. There are other block-piecing variations, but those two are the most common. Traditional blocks are pieced in either a clockwise or counterclockwise sequence. I usually piece my designs clockwise, but either way is correct. Courthouse Steps blocks are pieced with logs of equal size opposite each other, forming a symmetrical block.

Wherever I may use either block type in a quilt, I usually choose Courthouse Steps because this block is the fastest and easiest to speed-piece. Because the block is symmetrical, you can easily see where you are while you are constructing it, and the beginning step saves time; you join three strips instead of just the two you join for a Traditional block.

General Log Cabin Guidelines

- Trim selvages from strips.
- Use only straight, accurate strips. Discard or re-cut strips that are crooked or of incorrect width.
- Machine stitching should be straight and consistent, with ¼"-wide seam allowances. Set your machine for 12 to 14 stitches per inch and use neutral-colored thread.
- Press strips after each sewing step.

- Cut blocks apart accurately, removing any excess fabric between blocks.
- To keep block size consistent, do not change sewing machines, rulers, or methods in the middle of a project.
- When block centers are shapes other than squares or rectangles, maintain the correct angles by using the original center template rather than a ruler when cutting the blocks apart.

Traditional Blocks

To become familiar with speed piecing, use the block diagram below as if it were part of a pattern and make the blocks indicated. This example calls for "browns" and "whites," meaning you need several fabrics in each color group. Use several different white fabrics and brown fabrics in random order.

Make 6 Traditional blocks
(½ browns, ½ whites).

In the Traditional block, the smallest pieces—the center piece and the piece beside the center (brown piece #1 and white piece #2)—are squares.

1. Cut a 1"-wide strip of brown fabric and a 1"-wide strip of white fabric, each about 8" long (1" for each block plus a couple extra inches).
2. With right sides together, join the strips, using a ¼"-wide seam allowance. Press the seam allowance away from the center strip.
3. Cut the strip unit into 6 pieces, each 1" wide. Now you have pieces #1 and #2 sewn together for all 6 blocks.

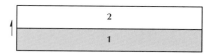

Press seams away from center square (brown).

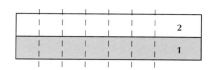

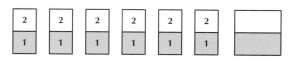

Excess

4. To add piece #3, lay a white strip on the sewing machine, right side up. Place the #1/#2 units on the strip, right sides down, with piece #2 of each unit closest to you. Sew along the right-hand edge, adding blocks as you sew. You may butt the blocks together on the strip, but do not overlap them.

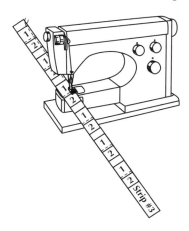

5. After sewing all 6 units to the strip, remove it from the machine. Press the seam allowance toward the new strip.
6. Cut the units apart, making sure to trim any excess fabric between the blocks. You now have 6 units that look like this:

7. To add piece #4, choose a strip of a different brown fabric than piece #1 and lay it on the sewing machine, right side up. Place the units on the strip, right sides down, with piece #3 closest to you. Sew the units to the strip.

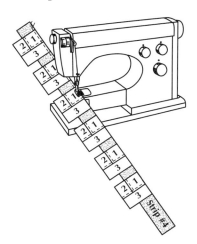

8. Press the seam allowances toward the new strip. Cut the units apart.

Repeat this process until all blocks have the required number of pieces.

Courthouse Steps Blocks

Unlike Traditional blocks, you do not place the piece added last nearest you. Always place Courthouse Steps blocks so you will be sewing across seams. Butt the blocks together as you place them on the strip, but do not overlap them.

Look at the Courthouse Steps sample, which calls for four blocks made of a variety of blue fabrics. Notice the center of the block: there are three small squares all the same size (pieces #1, #2, and #3).

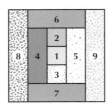

Courthouse Steps
Make 4 blocks
(all blues).

1. Select 3 different blue fabrics and cut a 1" x 6" strip from each (1" for each block, plus a couple extra inches). Sew the 3 strips together; press the seam allowances away from the center strip.

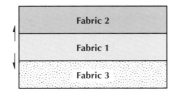

Press seams away from center strip.

2. Cut the strip into 4 pieces, each 1" wide. Now you have pieces #1, #2, and #3 sewn together for all 4 blocks.

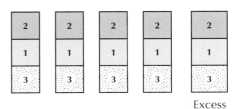

Excess

3. Select a strip of another blue for piece #4 (repeat a fabric if necessary). Lay the strip right side up on the sewing machine. Place the units right sides down on the strip. The units may be turned either way on the strip, with piece #2 or #3 at the top. Your design may require one placement or the other, but if fabric placement is not crucial to the design, varying the orientation will add more variety to the appearance of the blocks.

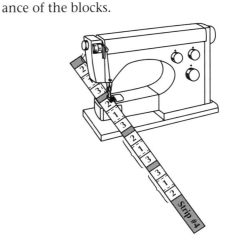

4. Press the seam allowances toward the new strip.
5. Cut the units apart, trimming any excess fabric between them.

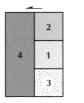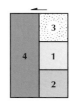

6. Select another blue strip for piece #5. Sew the units to the strip as shown. Press and cut the units apart.

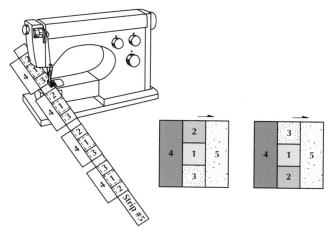

Repeat this process until all blocks have the required number of pieces.

Unusual and Non-Square Blocks

Sometimes a pattern calls for an unusual block. This means the pieces might be added out of order from the normal piecing sequence, or there may be an extra piece added to a log. Regardless of the piecing sequence, if you have more than one block of the same type, you may still use speed-piecing methods: placing the units on the strip and sewing them in groups.

Diamonds can be speed-pieced like squares. There are a few precautions, however. Think of the diamond as an arrow with a point at each end. When you begin sewing a series of diamonds onto a strip, you must leave extra room for the point at the start of the strip if the arrow at the seam line points up to the right as shown below (left). Diamonds may be butted together on the strip just like squares. Stitch along the edge. Leave room at the end of the strip if the arrow at the seam line points down to the right as shown below (right).

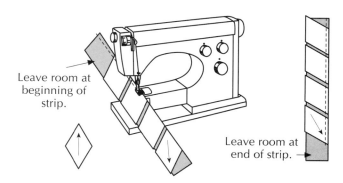

Leave room at beginning of strip.

Leave room at end of strip. →

Press the seam toward the strip and cut the blocks apart, using the diamond template to keep the angle true. Many rotary rulers have angle marks, but using an actual diamond template makes it much easier to be accurate.

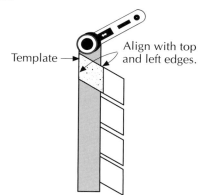

Template →

Align with top and left edges.

You can speed-piece triangles, but you must always leave room at the beginning and end of the strip, *and* between each triangle. Be sure to press seams toward the strip first, then use the triangle template to keep angles true as you cut the units apart. (The only exception is for triangles with an angle of 90° or greater.)

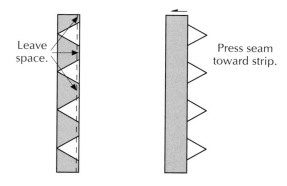

Leave space.

Press seam toward strip.

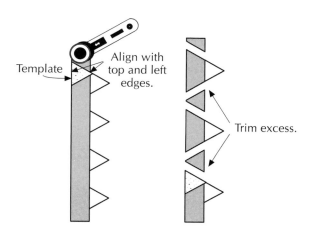

Template →

Align with top and left edges.

Trim excess.

Speed piecing hexagons is easy. No extra room on the strip is necessary. You can even overlap the blocks, as long as you don't stitch over two blocks at once. As with all other block types, press seams toward the strip, then use the template to keep the angles true as you cut the units apart.

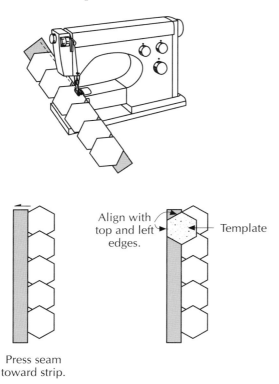

Align with top and left edges.

Template

Press seam toward strip.

Make a rounded block by simply stitching squares to the corners of a square block as if it were a Snowball block. Use squares the same width as the unsewn log strips. The fabric of the added squares should be the same color value as the next round of logs or the background to make the block appear rounded. Stitch the squares to the block, then trim away the triangles.

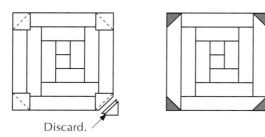

Discard.

To make a large number of Off-Center blocks (with logs on two sides only), make Courthouse Steps blocks with oversized center squares and cut them into four pieces. This will give you two each of two different kinds of Off-Center blocks.

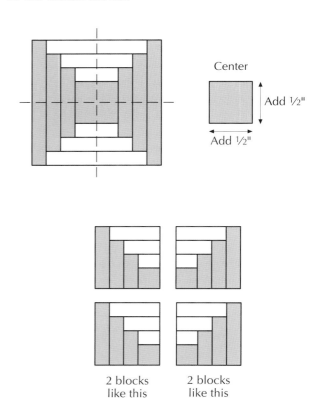

Center

Add 1/2"

Add 1/2"

2 blocks like this

2 blocks like this

Lopsided Log Cabin blocks are just as simple to make as normal Log Cabin blocks. The only difference is you cut strips of two widths instead of one.

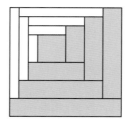

Add or omit chimneys as you add logs. To speed-piece, make a strip-pieced unit for each size log required.

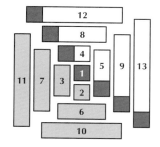

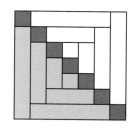

Construct the center of a two-directional Chimney and Cornerstones block as a nine-patch unit, then add cornerstones to the logs before stitching them to the block in Courthouse Steps fashion.

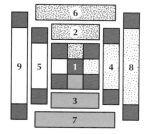

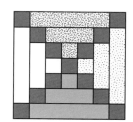

Use the same technique to make diamond Chimneys and Cornerstones blocks. Measure the correct angle from the fabric selvage to make a bias cut across the width of the fabric. The angle varies depending on the angle of the diamond. Cut a chimney strip the same width as the logs you plan to cut. Sew it to the bias edge of the fabric, trim the selvage, then crosscut into logs of the desired width.

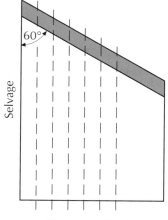

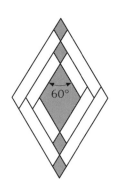

Crosscut strips for diamond cornerstones.

Troubleshooting

The following are some of the most common reasons for imperfect blocks.

- Strips cut unevenly cause misshapen blocks.
- Strips cut too wide or too narrow result in blocks that are too large or too small.
- Strips cut slightly on the bias and stretched during sewing or pressing create crooked blocks.
- Seam allowances too wide (more than ¼") or too narrow (less than ¼") cause blocks to be too large or too small.
- Inconsistent seam allowances cause blocks to bulge.
- A dull machine needle causes puckers and thread runs in the strips like runs in a nylon stocking.

- Faulty machine stitching may cause loose logs, tangles, or puckers.
- Failure to press between sewing steps or improper pressing can result in unwanted pleats.
- Steam pressing fabric that was not preshrunk may cause a block to shrink and distort.
- Using fabrics with different weights and textures may result in logs of varied widths.
- Failure to use the original template to cut apart unusual-shaped blocks can result in blocks that will not fit together properly.

To make "knots in the logs," piece strips together first, then crosscut the units into logs.

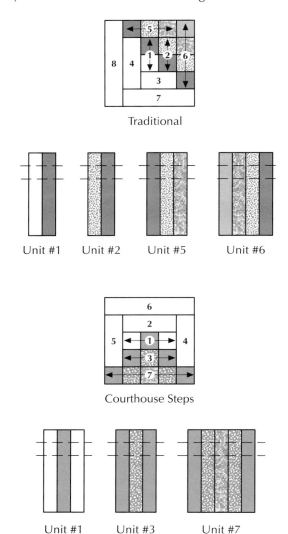

Traditional

Unit #1   Unit #2   Unit #5   Unit #6

Courthouse Steps

Unit #1   Unit #3   Unit #7

Each block for "Pleated Sunshine and Shadows" (page 93) was pieced on a foundation layered with batting and backing—a cumbersome, time-consuming method. I devised a way to make Semi-Pleated blocks, in which every other round of logs is pleated. They look like the antique blocks, but are lighter weight and faster and easier to make. You can make any block shape this way.

Piece the block in the usual manner through the first complete round of logs (piece #5). After adding the first log of round 2 (piece #6), pleat that log by pressing the raw edge even with the raw edge of the last round. Pleat each log of round 2 after you sew it to the block.

As you add the third round of logs (pieces #10–#13), press each log as you would a normal block.

Continue pleating every *other* round, but begin and end the block with *unpleated* rounds. Otherwise, the block edge will be thick and difficult to join to the next block. The only difference between the Semi-Pleated block and a normal block is this simple pressing step in every other round of logs.

1st round—
normal piecing

2nd round—
Add piece #6...

then press raw
edges even with
edge of round 1.

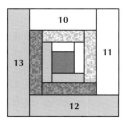

Press pleats in
pieces #7, #8,
and #9.

Press normally for
round 3 (pieces #10,
#11, #12, and #13).

To make a three-dimensional, Semi-Pleated block, tack the pleated logs back as shown so they look like blooming petals.

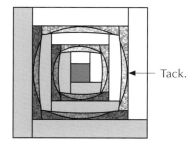

Tack.

The diagrams for the alphabet and number blocks show the piecing sequences. Cut piece #1 the specified size, then follow the piecing sequence, adding strips in numerical order. Cut all strips for these blocks 1" wide.

Alphabet and Number Blocks

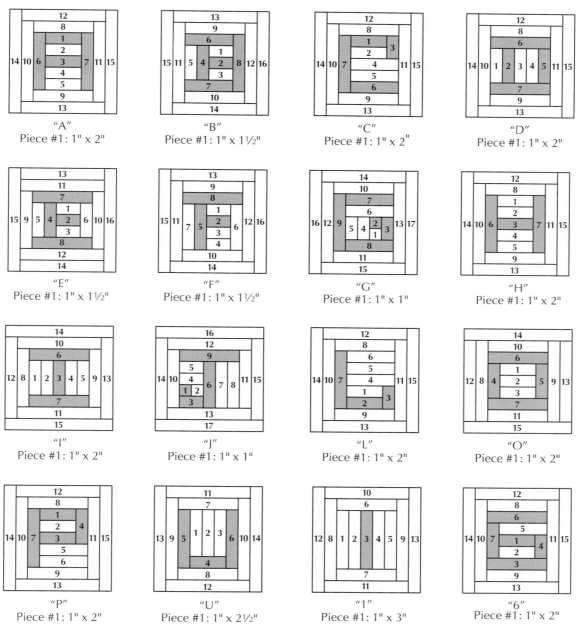

Alphabet and Number Blocks (continued)

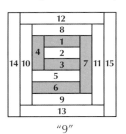

"8"
Piece #1: 1" x 2"

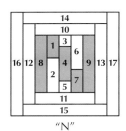

"9"
Piece #1: 1" x 2"

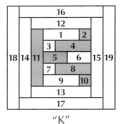

"K"
#1 (2") to #2 (1")
#3 (1") to #4 (2")
#5 (1½") to #6 (1½")
#7 (1") to #8 (2")
#9 (2") to #10 (1")

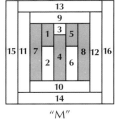

"M"
#1 (1½") to #2 (2")
#3 (1") to #4 (2½")
#5 (1½") to #6 (2")
Sew these together,
then add #7, and so on.

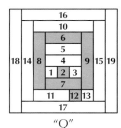

"N"
#1 (1½") to #2 (2")
#3 (1") to #4 (2") to #5 (1")
#6 (2") to #7 (1½")
Sew these together, then
add #8, and so on.

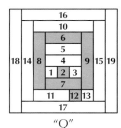

"Q"
#1 (1") to #2 (1") to #3 (1"
#11 (2") to #12 (1") to #13 (
Sew unit 1/2/3 to piece #4
and so on.

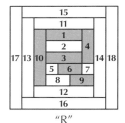

"R"
#1,#2, #3 (2") #5 (1") to
#6 (1½") to #7 (1")
#8 (1½") to #9 (1½")
Sew pieces 1–4 in order, add
unit 5/6/7, then unit 8/9,
and so on.

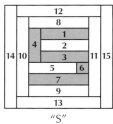

"S"
#1, #2, #3 (2½")
#5 (2½") to #6 (1")
Sew pieces 1–4 in
order, add unit 5/6, and
continue in order.

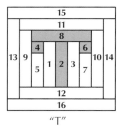

"T"
#1, #2, #3 (2½")
#4 (1") to #5 (2")
#6 (1") to #7 (2")
Sew pieces 1–3, then
add unit 4/5 and unit
6/7; continue piecing
in order.

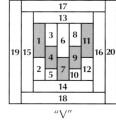

"V"
#1 (2") to #2 (1½")
#3 (1½") to #4 (1½") to #5 (
#6 (2") to #7 (1½")
#8 (1½") to #9 (1½") to #10
#11 (2") to #12 (1½")
Piece units together;
continue piecing in order

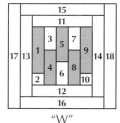

"W"
#1 (2½") to #2 (1")
#3 (1½") to #4 (2")
#5 (2") to #6 (1½")
#7 (1½") to #8 (2")
#9 (2½") to #10 (1")
Sew units together and
continue piecing in order.

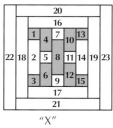

"X"
#1 (1") to #2 (2") to #3 (1")
#4 (1½") to #5 (1") to #6 (1½")
#7 (1") to #8 (2") to #9 (1")
#10 (1½") to #11 (1") to #12 (1½")
#13 (1") to #14 (2") to #15 (1")
Sew units together and
continue piecing in order.

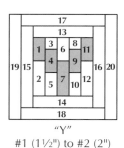

"Y"
#1 (1½") to #2 (2")
#3 (1") to #4 (1½") to #5 (1½")
#6 (1½") to #7 (2")
#8 (1") to #9 (1½") to #10 (1 ½")
#11 (1½") to #12 (2")
#13 (1") to #14 (2") to #15 (1")
Sew units together and
continue piecing in order.

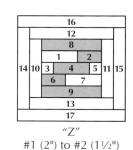

"Z"
#1 (2") to #2 (1½")
#3 (1") to #4 (2") to #5 (1"
#6 (1½") to #7 (2")
Sew units together and
continue piecing in order

Alphabet and Number Blocks (continued)

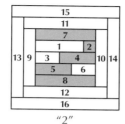

"2"
#1 (2½") to #2 (1")
#3 (1½") to #4 (2")
#5 (2") to #6 (1½")
Sew units together and
continue piecing in order.

"3"
#1 (2½") to #2 (1")
#3 (1½") to #4 (2")
#5 (2½") to #6 (1")
Sew units together and
continue piecing in order.

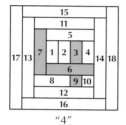

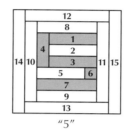

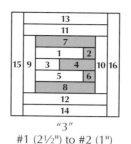

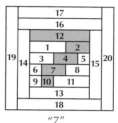

"4"
#1, #2, #3, #4 (1½")
#8 (2") to #9 (1") to #10 (1")
Sew pieces 1–7, then add
unit 8/9/10, and continue
piecing in order.

"5"
#1, #2, #3 (2½")
#5 (2½") to #6 (1")
Sew pieces 1–4, then add
unit 5/6, and continue
piecing in order.

"7"
#1 (2") to #2 (1½")
#3 (1½") to #4 (1½") to #5 (1")
#6 (1") to #7 (1½") to #8 (1½")
#9 (1") to #10 (1") to #11 (2")
Sew units together and
continue piecing in order.

Assembling the Quilt

Complete all the blocks for a project before sewing them together. Always match blocks at the seams before joining them. If the blocks do not match exactly, you can sometimes stretch the smaller block slightly to fit. If there is too much difference for them to match, you may have to adjust or even remake a block.

It is often important to decide whether to assemble square blocks in horizontal or vertical rows. For example, look at "Strawberries and Tea" (page 90).

Notice that the blocks must match perfectly in places where colors connect, such as the red bands on the cups and teapot. In this example, horizontal connections are more important than vertical ones. Assemble this pattern in horizontal rows to ensure accurate connections when the rows are joined.

When you join horizontal rows of blocks, alternate the pressing; that is, press the seams in row 1 to the right, in row 2 to the left, in row 3 to the right, and so on. For vertical rows, press the seams in row 1 up, in row 2 down, in row 3 up, and so on. When you join the rows, the seam allowances will lie in opposite directions and butt up against each other snugly. The long seams between rows may be pressed in either direction.

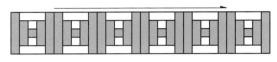

Row #1
Press seams to right.

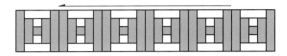

Row #2
Press seams to left.

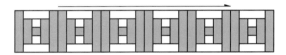

Row #3
Press seams to right.

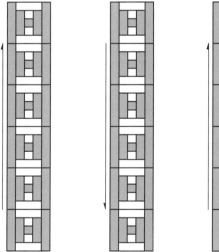

Row #1
Press seams up.
Row #2
Press seams down.
Row #3
Press seams up.

Setting in Blocks

If the block shape is hexagonal, diamond shaped, or any other shape that must be set in, use the following method.

1. Mark a dot at the seam intersection of each block point. With right sides together, match points with pins and stitch from point to point, leaving seam allowances unsewn.

2. Set in outer blocks or pieces by matching seam intersections and stitching one side at a time, from the seam intersection outward. Be sure to keep seam allowances away from the stitching line so you are never sewing through more than 2 layers.

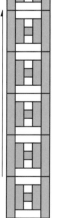

Log Cabin Design Grids

The following pages of Log Cabin block grids may be photocopied. Use them to color in quilt designs, to design unusual blocks, or to cut blocks apart and paste them together in new ways.

Traditional blocks (9 pieces, 2 rounds of logs)

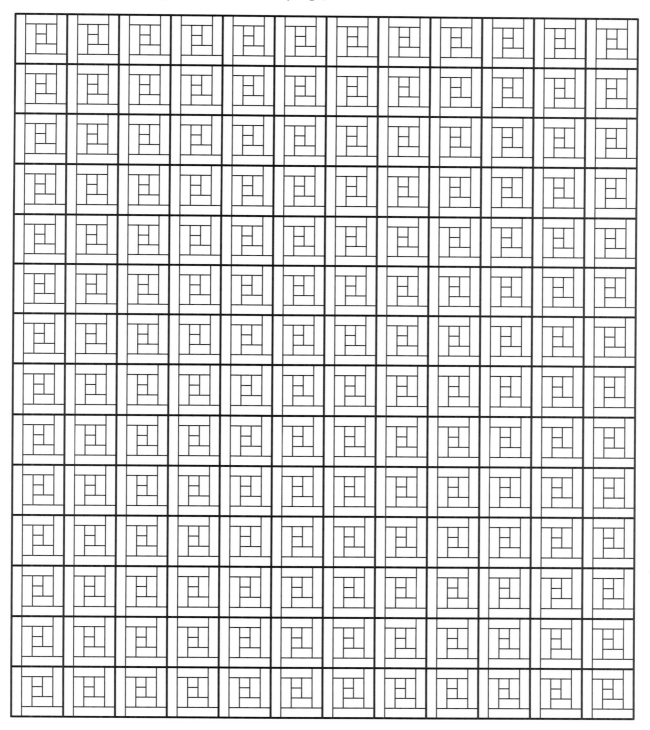

Courthouse Steps blocks (9 pieces, 2 rounds of logs)

Traditional blocks (13 pieces, 3 rounds of logs)

Courthouse Steps blocks (13 pieces, 3 rounds of logs)

Traditional blocks (17 pieces, 4 rounds of logs)

Courthouse Steps blocks (17 pieces, 4 rounds of logs)

Equilateral Triangle Grid

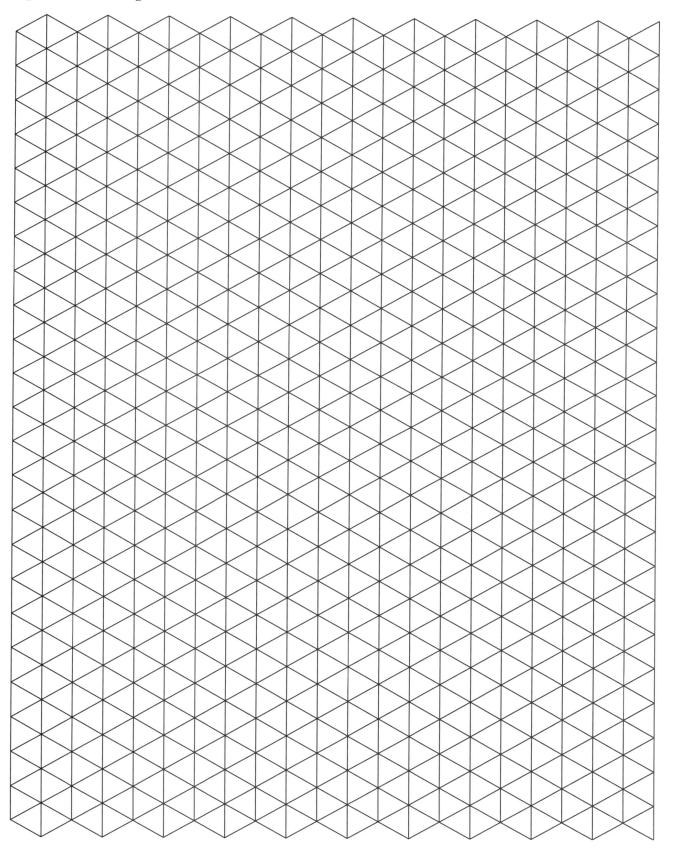

Traditional equilateral triangles (7 pieces, 2 rounds of logs)

Traditional 60° diamonds (9 pieces, 2 rounds of logs)

Courthouse Steps 60° diamonds (9 pieces, 2 rounds of logs)

Traditional hexagons (13 pieces, 2 rounds of logs)

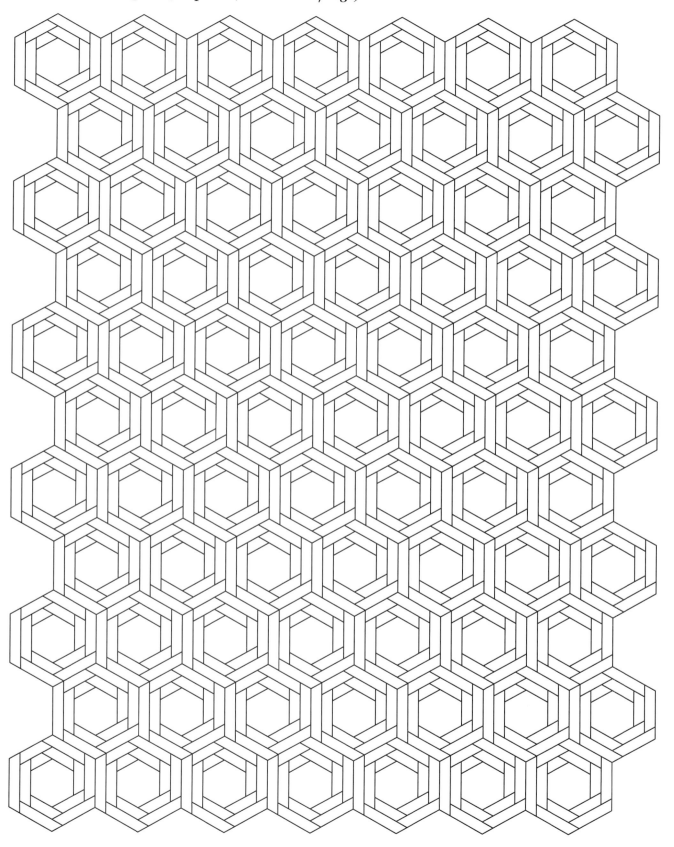

Courthouse Steps hexagons (13 pieces, 2 rounds of logs)

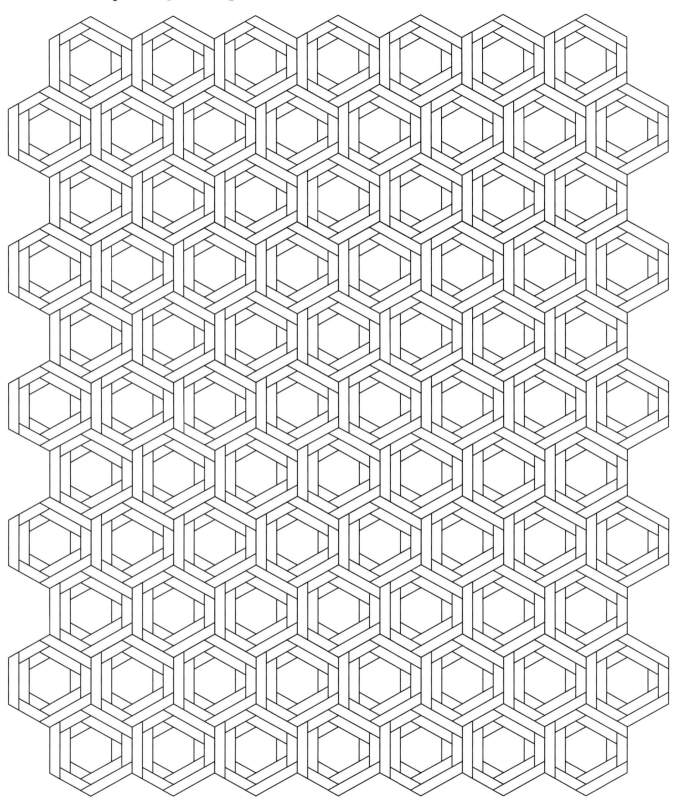

Gallery of Quilts

CHINESE DRAGON DANCE *by Vicky Haider, 46" x 46". This beautiful dragon, appliquéd over a Split Log Cabin background, was designed by a student in North Dakota. Vicky combined squares and diamonds for the background of this Asian-theme quilt. The script in silver lamé spells "Chinese Dragon Dance."*

ELEPHANT WALK *by Christal Carter, 73" x 83". This jungle sampler has hexagon Log Cabin blocks with fussy-cut diamond centers. A star is formed by adding triangle Log Cabin blocks to the hexagon blocks. The spaces between the star tips are filled with Diamond Log Cabin blocks containing chimneys and cornerstones. The borders showcase elephants with appliquéd palm leaves, and a tiny elephant print binds the edges.*

CHIMNEYS AND CORNERSTONES II *by Christal Carter, 34" x 34". This quilt breaks the traditional look of the block with a center chimney of a different size and color than the cornerstones, bringing a more contemporary look to the piece. Notice that some of the blocks invade the border for interest.*

STRAWBERRIES AND TEA *by Christal Carter, 39" x 26½". A Log Cabin pictorial design like this is fun to create and easy to sew. Both basic block types are used, and the strawberry and handle details are appliquéd.*

LOG CABIN IN THE WOODS *by Christal Carter, 33" x 33". This small, felt quilt is hand pieced and appliquéd with pearl cotton. The central Log Cabin blocks were first fused to the background, then hand stitched. The raw edges were simply butted together. The log cabin and pines were appliquéd over the blocks. Animals and trees native to the California mountains surround the cabin section.*

HEXAGON TABLE TOPPER *by Christal Carter, 29" x 33". Seven Hexagon blocks are framed by six diamonds to create this pretty little tabletop quilt.*

SPOOL BOX *by Christal Carter, 40" x 37". This quilt was designed not only to use up scrap fabric but also to showcase a Courthouse Steps variation. Each block center is a rectangle of pieced strips. The center of the quilt is a giant Courthouse Steps block.*

HOLLY AND THE IVY *by Christal Carter, 42" x 48". This quilt was inspired by a small etching in a girl's scrapbook from 1898. The central figure, Holly, and the cluster of ivy leaves are hand appliquéd and embroidered over Split Log Courthouse Steps blocks. The background quilting design makes the blocks less obvious but adds texture to the quilt. Sawed Log blocks, alternating with half Snowball blocks, make an easy scalloped border around the poinsettia print fabric.*

GRANDMA'S REALLY COOKIN' *by Christal Carter, 43" x 54". This unusual Courthouse Steps variation forms a Streak of Lightning setting, which is usually created only with Traditional Log Cabin blocks. Offsetting the blocks forms the characteristic zigzags. The block centers are all different shapes and sizes. I added logs of varying widths to make all blocks the same size. Appliquéd cookies, rolling pin, and frosting add to the fun.*

ROSEGAY PILLOW *by Christal Carter, 18" x 18". Rounded Log Cabin blocks form a nosegay of roses on a romantic pillow. Three-dimensional "bumps on a log" leaves are tucked into the logs. See page 15.*

ON STAGE *by Christal Carter, 41" x 41". This quilt was made for my daughter when she starred in a college production of "Quilters." It features the ever-popular Barn Raising setting with appliquéd comic and tragic masks.*

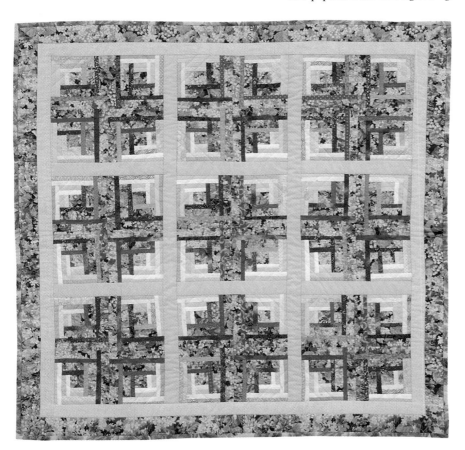

WOVEN HYDRANGEAS *by Christal Carter, 50" x 50". These lopsided blocks resemble large hydrangea blooms woven with red and gold ribbons. The Split Log blocks contain logs of varying sizes, creating the lopsided appearance and making the floral areas seem rounded.*

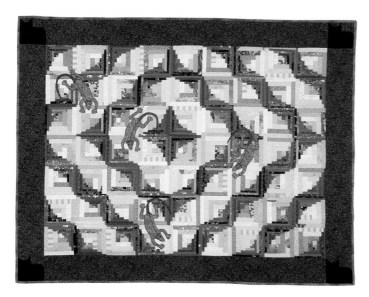

CAT FOOD *by Deborah Myers, 57" x 70". Debbie's title for this quilt came from observing her nephew's chameleons, who attempt to survive in a house with five cats! The quilt features Lopsided blocks in a Barn Raising variation. The lizards are appliquéd, and the cats in the borders are pieced.*

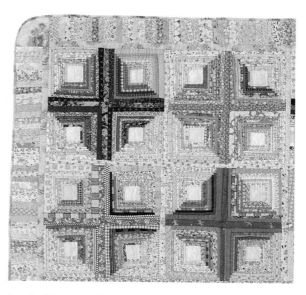

Detail of **PLEATED SUNSHINE AND SHADOWS** *by Christal Carter, 46" x 46". I used vintage fabrics to complete this foundation-pieced quilt from a set of unfinished blocks. Working with these blocks led me to devise the easier Semi-Pleated block method on page 72.*

TOYTIME TEDDY *by Christal Carter, 82" x 92". This 5,000-piece pictorial quilt features a giant teddy bear sitting among his toys. The alphabet and numerals, made of Log Cabin variations, show just how flexible the block can be. See pages 73–75 for the alphabet.*

I LOVE A LOG CABIN *by Christal Carter, 56" x 74". Quilted by Barbara Ford. I use this quilt in my "Splitting Logs" workshops to illustrate spiraled Courthouse Steps, Hexagon, Triangle, Semi-Pleated, Sawed Log, Split Log, rounded Spiral, alphabet, "knots in the log," Diamond, Lopsided, Off-Center, small pictorial, as well as Traditional and Courthouse Steps blocks. The snail with thread and thimble is my logo.*

TICKER TAPE *by Christal Carter, 42" x 56". Half-square triangles in celebration colors form the centers of these easy triangle Log Cabin blocks. Black prints include balloons, hats, cars, and curlicues of thread to mimic a ticker-tape parade. The colorful rectangle border is a geometric print fabric.*

COMPASS IN THE CABIN *by Christal Carter, 81" x 81". Quilted by Barbara Ford. Traditional and Courthouse Steps blocks combine to make the star and border around a central Mariner's Compass block. The beige border blocks appear rectangular due to the addition of blue logs on the block sides.*

RESURRECTION *by Christal Carter, 72" x 96". Designed in 1982, this was my first sampler Log Cabin quilt. Made as an Easter quilt, it features several variations of five different Log Cabin shapes: squares, rectangles, triangles, diamonds, and hexagons. To soften the many sharp angles, the corded border is curved.*

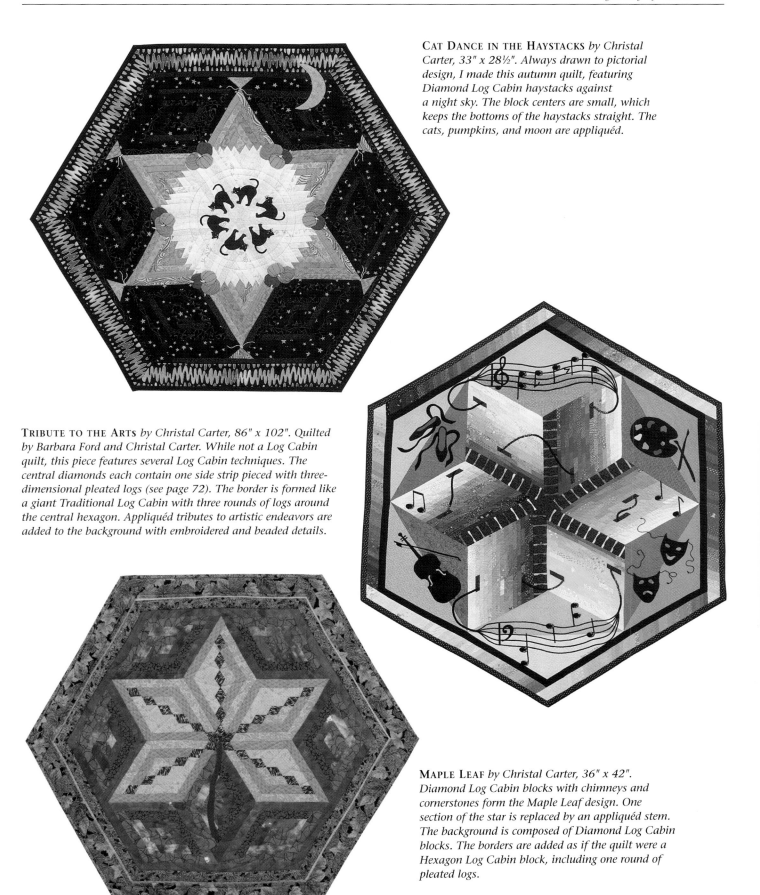

CAT DANCE IN THE HAYSTACKS *by Christal Carter, 33" x 28½". Always drawn to pictorial design, I made this autumn quilt, featuring Diamond Log Cabin haystacks against a night sky. The block centers are small, which keeps the bottoms of the haystacks straight. The cats, pumpkins, and moon are appliquéd.*

TRIBUTE TO THE ARTS *by Christal Carter, 86" x 102". Quilted by Barbara Ford and Christal Carter. While not a Log Cabin quilt, this piece features several Log Cabin techniques. The central diamonds each contain one side strip pieced with three-dimensional pleated logs (see page 72). The border is formed like a giant Traditional Log Cabin with three rounds of logs around the central hexagon. Appliquéd tributes to artistic endeavors are added to the background with embroidered and beaded details.*

MAPLE LEAF *by Christal Carter, 36" x 42". Diamond Log Cabin blocks with chimneys and cornerstones form the Maple Leaf design. One section of the star is replaced by an appliquéd stem. The background is composed of Diamond Log Cabin blocks. The borders are added as if the quilt were a Hexagon Log Cabin block, including one round of pleated logs.*

U.F.O. *by Nancy Ota, 56" x 47". Begun in workshops by June Ryker, this wonderful Log Cabin quilt features several different block types. Notice the curved, pie-shaped blocks that June Ryker devised using paper piecing. Nancy titled the quilt "U.F.O." because it looks like an unidentified flying object and also because it remained an "UnFinished Object" for some time!*

GALLOPING MEMORIES *by Barbara Ford, 55" x 55". Barbara designed this lovely Barn Raising Log Cabin quilt. Each hand-appliquéd figure represents a horse Barbara has owned and loved. The red barn, pieced of ¼" strips, sits in a field of snow. The border fence completes this wintry scene.*

JOY RIDING *by Christal Carter, 47" x 55". Inspired by the family photograph of a close friend, I designed this pictorial appliqué in sepia-toned fabrics. The quilt looked unfinished until I added some Split Log Cabin borders, which gave the piece additional size and a warm and friendly aged look. Hand appliquéd and embroidered.*